My Book

This book belongs to

Name:_____

1

2   www.math-knots.com | www.a4ace.com

Cover Design by :
Gowri Vemuri

First Edition :
August , 2023

Author :
Gowri Vemuri

Edited by :
Raksha Pothapragada

Questions: mathknots.help@gmail.com

NOTE : CCSSO or NCTM or VDOE is neither affiliated nor sponsors or endorses this product.

Dedication

This book is dedicated to:

My Mom, who is my best critic, guide and supporter.

To what I am today, and what I am going to become tomorrow,

is all because of your blessings, unconditional affection and support.

This book is dedicated to the

strongest women of my life ,

my dearest mom

and

to all those moms in this universe.

G.V.

5

Week	Page No
Week 1	11-22
Week 2	23-38
Week 3	39-52
Week 4	53-68
Answer Keys	69-113

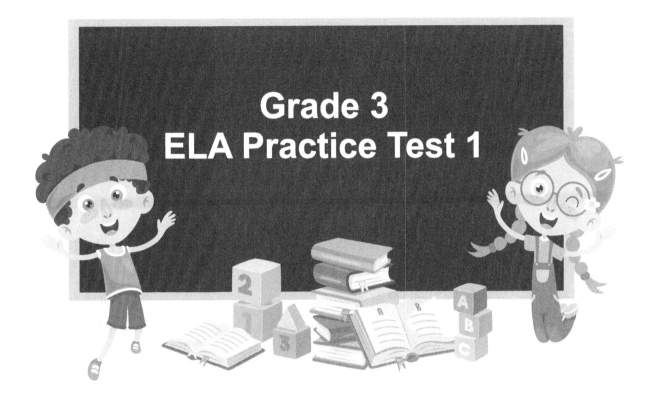

Grade 3
ELA Practice Test 1

Directions: *Read the passages and answer the questions that follow.*

Long the Dragon: Bringing Luck and Good Fortune

1. Long ago in China, there was a dragon named Long. He was known as the most powerful and divine creature in all of China. The dragons were the symbol of the emperor, bringing luck and good fortune. Long loved to help the people of China with his amazing powers. He could control the water, make it rain, and even bring good luck to the farmers' crops.

2. One day, a terrible drought hit the land. The crops were dying, and the people were starting to worry. Long knew he had to do something to help. He flew to the sky and gathered all the clouds he could find. Then he used all his power to make it rain.

3. The rain fell on the land, and soon the crops started to grow again. The people of China were so thankful to Long for his help. They knew he was the hero of their land and the symbol of good fortune.

4. After he had helped the people, Long turned into a dragonfly and flew into the heavens. But he would always be remembered as the mighty dragon who helped bring good luck and fortune to the people of China.

- Adapted from Chinese mythology

1. What was Long's special ability?

A. Controlling the wind

B. Making it snow

C. Controlling water

D. Controlling fire

2. What does the word "divine" mean in this passage?

A. Powerful

B. Holy

C. Mythical

D. Helpful

3. Why were the people of China thankful to Long?

A. He controlled the wind

B. He made it rain

C. He brought good luck to their crops

D. All of the above

4. What happened to the crops when the drought hit the land?

    A. They grew faster

    B. They got bigger

    C. They started to die

    D. They were moved to a different location

5. What does the word "drought" mean in this passage?

    A. Heavy rain

    B. Dry spell

    C. Cold weather

    D. Forest fire

6. How did Long leave after helping the people?

    A. He left on a boat

    B. He disappeared into thin air

    C. He went back to his cave

    D. He turned into a smaller creature and flew into the heavens

7. Which of the following best describes Long's role in China?

    A. He was a powerful dragon who controlled the water and brought

        good luck and fortune.

    B. He was a heroic farmer who saved the crops during a drought.

    C. He was a symbol of the emperor and brought rain to the land.

    D. He was a dragonfly who flew into the heavens after helping the people.

8. What role did dragons play in Chinese culture?

    A. Dragons were the rulers of China.

    B. Dragons were the protectors of the emperor.

    C. Dragons were symbols of luck and good fortune.

    D. Dragons were mythical creatures that brought destruction.

9. **Which word in the passage best defines the meaning of the prefix**

   "re-" in the word "remembered"?

   A. Forget   B. Repeat

   C. Repair   D. Remove

The Boy Who Cried Wolf

Once upon a time, there was a young boy named Jack who lived in a village with his parents. Jack's job was to watch over his family's sheep, making sure they were safe from wolves and other predators. One day, Jack got bored and decided to play a trick on the villagers. He ran into the village shouting, "Wolf, wolf! A wolf is attacking my sheep!"

The villagers ran to help Jack, but when they got to the field, they found no wolf. Jack laughed and said, "Ha! I fooled you all!" The next day, Jack repeated his prank. The villagers were annoyed but still came to help. After several times, the villagers stopped believing Jack.

One day, a real wolf attacked Jack's sheep and Jack cried out for help, but the villagers did not believe him. As a result, the wolf ate several of his sheep. Jack learned an important lesson that day – his lies had cost him the trust of the villagers. From then on, he promised never to lie again and to always be truthful so that others could trust him.

-Adapted from The boy who cried wolf From Aesop's Fables

10. **What was Jack's job?**

   A. To watch over his family's pigs

   B. To watch over his family's sheep

   C. To watch over his family's horses

11. **What does the word "treacherous" mean in the context of the story?**

   A. dangerous and hazardous

   B. friendly and welcoming

   C. peaceful and serene

12. **What happened when a real wolf attacked Jack's sheep?**

   A. The villagers believed Jack and helped him protect his sheep

   B. The villagers did not believe Jack and the wolf ate several of his sheep

   C. Jack was able to protect all of his sheep from the wolf

13. Which word in the story means "to prevent or stop from happening"?

A. Thwart

B. Wane

C. Fortify

14. Why did Jack decide to play a trick on the villagers?

A. He was bored

B. He wanted to make them angry

C. He was hungry

15. What did Jack shout when he ran into the village?

A. "Bear, bear! A bear is attacking my sheep!"

B. "Tiger, tiger! A tiger is attacking my sheep!"

C. "Wolf, wolf! A wolf is attacking my sheep!"

16. How did the villagers feel after Jack played his trick on them several times?

A. Happy

B. Annoyed

C. Excited

17. What lesson did Jack learn from the experience?

A. To always play tricks on people

B. That it is okay to lie to get attention

C. That being truthful is important for others to trust you.

Jimia's Brave Adventure

1. Jimia was a third-grade student who had a secret fear: she was scared of heights. Whenever she had to climb even a small ladder or go near a balcony, her heart would race, and her legs would tremble. Jimia felt frustrated and wished she could be as brave as her friends.

2. One sunny day, Jimia's class planned a field trip to the local adventure park. Jimia was excited but also nervous. The park had a high rope course that challenged people to overcome their fears. Jimia knew this was her chance to conquer her fear of heights.

3. As they arrived at the park, Jimia could see the tall towers and wobbly bridges of the rope course. Her hands felt sweaty, but she took a deep breath and decided to give it a try. With the support of her classmates and the encouraging words from her teacher, Jimia climbed up the ladder and started navigating the course.

4. With every step, her confidence grew. She faced her fear head-on, one obstacle at a time. Jimia's friends cheered her on, and soon enough, she reached the final platform. From up there, Jimia looked down and smiled. She had done it!

5. As Jimia climbed back down, she felt proud and accomplished. She realized that being brave was not about never being scared but facing fears with courage. From that day forward, Jimia was determined to take on new challenges and embrace her bravery.

18. In paragraph 2, what did Jimia's class plan for their field trip?

    A. Going to the zoo

    B. Visiting a museum

    C. Going to an adventure park

    D. Watching a movie

19. According to paragraph 3, what was Jimia scared of?

    A. Water

    B. Animals

    C. Heights

    D. Darkness

20. In which paragraph did Jimia climb up the ladder to start the rope course?

    A. Paragraph 2

    B. Paragraph 3

    C. Paragraph 4

    D. Paragraph 5

21. What helped Jimia gather the courage to start the rope course,

    as mentioned in paragraph 4?

    A. The support of her classmates and teacher

    B. Seeing her friends complete the course

    C. A magic potion she drank

    D. Her favorite music playing in the background

22. According to paragraph 5, how did Jimia feel as she faced each obstacle

    in the rope course?

    A. She became more scared

    B. She gave up and went back down

www.math-knots.com | www.a4ace.com

C. Her confidence grew

D. She asked for help from her teacher

23. In which paragraph did Jimia's friends cheer her on as she navigated the rope course?

    A. Paragraph 2

    B. Paragraph 3

    C. Paragraph 4

    D. Paragraph 5

24. How did Jimia feel after conquering her fear, as mentioned in paragraph 5?

    A. Angry

    B. Proud and accomplished

    C. Disappointed

    D. Sad and scared

25. What did Jimia realize about being brave, as mentioned in paragraph 5?

    A. It meant never feeling scared

    B. It meant avoiding challenges

    C. It meant facing fears with courage

    D. It meant always winning

26. In which paragraph did Jimia reach the final platform of the rope course?

    A. Paragraph 2

    B. Paragraph 3

    C. Paragraph 4

    D. Paragraph 5

How The Camel Got His Hump

1. Once upon a time, in the early days of the world, there lived a Camel in the middle of a vast desert. This Camel was quite different from the other animals. He was lazy and didn't want to work. In fact, he was known for his howling sounds. Instead of doing any useful tasks, he would eat sticks, thorns, tamarisks, and prickles, doing absolutely nothing productive. Whenever anyone tried to talk to him, all he would say was, "Humph!" and nothing more.

2. One Monday morning, the Horse approached the Camel with a saddle on his back and a bit in his mouth, urging him to come out and trot like the rest of them. But the Camel simply responded with his usual "Humph!" The disappointed Horse went and reported the matter to the Man.

www.math-knots.com | www.a4ace.com

3. Soon after, the Dog came to the Camel carrying a stick, insisting that he should come and fetch and carry like the others. Again, the Camel replied with a lazy "Humph!" The Dog, too, went and informed the Man about the Camel's refusal.

4. Next, the Ox approached the Camel with a yoke on his neck, inviting him to come and plow like the rest. But the Camel, as always, responded with a nonchalant "Humph!" The Ox went and reported the matter to the Man.

5. At the end of the day, the Man called the Horse, the Dog, and the Ox together. He expressed his regret, for the world was new and needed everyone's contribution. However, he acknowledged that the Camel was an idle creature and could not be forced to work. As a result, he instructed the Horse, the Dog, and the Ox to work twice as hard to make up for the Camel's laziness.

6. This decision angered the Horse, the Dog, and the Ox. They held a meeting on the edge of the desert, discussing the matter. Meanwhile, the Camel continued his idle ways, chewing on milkweed and mocking the others with his "Humph!" Then, a Djinn, who was in charge of all the deserts, appeared in a cloud of dust. The Horse approached the Djinn and voiced his concern about the Camel's idleness, asking if it was right for anyone to be so lazy in a new world.

7. The Djinn, in agreement, became curious and identified the Camel as the culprit. The Horse mentioned the Camel's unhelpful response, and the Dog and the Ox added that he wouldn't fetch, carry, or plow either. The Djinn decided to take matters into his own hands. As a punishment, the Camel was made to carry a hump on his back.

-Adapted from How The Camel Got His Hump by Rudyard Kipling

27. What was the Camel known for among the animals?

    A. Working hard

    B. Making loud howling sounds

    C. Helping others

    D. Eating grass

28. Why did the Horse approach the Camel?

    A. To challenge him to a race

    B. To ask for a ride

    C. To invite him to trot like the others

    D. To complain about the weather

29. Who else tried to persuade the Camel to work?

    A. The Dog

    B. The Owl

    C. The Djinn

D. The Man

30. What did the Camel say when asked to plow like the rest?

    A. "I'm ready!"

    B. "Humph!"

    C. "I don't know how."

    D. "Let's get started!"

31. Why did the Man instruct the Horse, the Dog, and the Ox to work twice as hard?

    A. Because the Camel was their friend

    B. Because they wanted to impress the Djinn

    C. Because the world was new and needed everyone's contribution

    D. Because they were the strongest animals

32. Who appeared in a cloud of dust to address the Camel's laziness?

    A. The Djinn

    B. The Man

    C. The Horse

    D. The Dog

33. What consequence did the Camel face for his idle behavior?

    A. He was banished from the desert.

    B. He had to carry a hump on his back.

    C. He became the leader of the other animals.

    D. He was given a reward for his laziness.

34. Which sentence from the story of the Camel suggests that the Camel was not willing to work?

    A. "All he would say was, "Humph!" and nothing more."

    B. "The Horse approached the Camel with a saddle on his back."

    C. "The Dog came to the Camel carrying a stick."

    D. "The Ox approached the Camel with a yoke on his neck."

35. Which question is answered in paragraph 2 of the story of the Camel?

    A. Why did the Horse approach the Camel?

    B. What did the Djinn do when he saw the Camel?

    C. Where did the Horse, the Dog, and the Ox meet?

    D. Who discovered the Camel's laziness?

The Mysterious Move and the Curious Imp

Celeste and her mother Hannah were headed toward their new home in Cripley Hollow.

"Are you all, right? Hannah asked.

Celeste nodded. She was excited to be going to a new place, but she was also a little afraid.

But this is until she sees the house. It is a run-down ramshackle place that could use wrecking ball more than a mop.
And Celeste is not the only one unhappy about the move.
Grumblemunch the imp has lived in the cellar of the old house for decades. He loves the junk he has collected, and he enjoys running through the tall grass. Now, all that is changing.

Earlier that morning, a rumbling woke Grumblemunch the imp from his sleep way too early.
Grumblemunch peered out and blinked in the bright sunlight. The rumbling come from the yard and shook the ground, but the Imp could not see what was causing it.
A streak of orange bolting past him knocked Grumblemunch against the door.

36. How does Celeste feel about the house she is supposed to move into?

    A. Excited

    B. Happy

    C. Unhappy

    D. None of the above

37. What could the house use instead of just a mop?

    A. New windows

    B. A fresh coat of paint

    C. A wrecking ball

    D. A new kitchen

38. Why does Celeste's mother want her to move to Cripley Hollow?

    A. She got a new job there

    B. She wants a fresh start

    C. She inherited the house from a relative

    D. None of the above

39. Who else is unhappy about the move besides Celeste?

    A. Celeste's father

    B. Grumblemunch

    C. Celeste's sister

    D. All of the above

40. Where does Grumblemunch live in the old house?

    A. The basement

B. The attic

C. The backyard

D. The shed

41. What does Grumblemunch love to collect?

    A. Rocks

    B. Books

    C. Junk

    D. None of the above

42. What does Grumblemunch like to do in the tall grass?

    A. chase butterflies   B. eat insects

    C. running around   D. none of the above

43. Why is everything changing for Grumblemunch?

    A. His favorite tree was cut down

    B. New people are moving into the house

    C. His collection got ruined

    D. All of the above

Weaving of Kente Cloth Taught by a Spider

1. Kente cloth is a highly revered and symbolic fabric, known for its intricate patterns and vibrant colors. Kente cloth is a type of silk and cotton fabric made of interwoven cloth strips and is native to the Akan ethnic group. This unique cloth holds significant cultural and historical importance, with a legend that dates back approximately 375 years.

2. According to the legend, two brothers named Kurugu and Ameyaw went on a hunting expedition in the small city of Bonwire. During their journey, they came across a remarkable sight—a spider meticulously weaving an extraordinary web. Mesmerized by the spider's intricate work, the brothers carefully observed the details and mechanics of the weaving process.

3. Inspired by the spider's craftsmanship, Kurugu and Ameyaw returned to their community with newfound knowledge. They set out to replicate the weaving technique they had witnessed, using fibers obtained from the raffia tree. Combining black and white fibers, they skillfully created their first cloth, which would eventually become the precursor to the renowned Kente cloth.

4. Over time, Kente cloth gained immense popularity and became associated with the Akan people's royalty and cultural heritage. The fabric's significance extended beyond mere adornment, as it held sacred and ceremonial value. In the past, Kente cloth was exclusively reserved for special occasions and festivities, and only kings had the privilege of wearing it.

5. This cloth used to be woven by only men as it was believed that a girl's growing up years could interfere with its production. As time progressed, the production of Kente cloth changed from being just the domain of men. Women gradually became involved in the weaving process, contributing their skills and creativity to the art form. Today, Kente cloth continues to be revered and cherished, not only in Ghana but also across the

20

world, as a symbol of African culture, craftsmanship, and tradition. Its vibrant colors, intricate designs, and rich history make it a truly remarkable textile.

44. What is Kente cloth made of?

    A. Silk and cotton

    B. Wool and linen

    C. Polyester and nylon

    D. Velvet and silk

45. What did the brothers use to make their first cloth?

    A. Black and white fibers

    B. Silk and cotton threads

    C. Raffia tree leaves

    D. Spider silk

46. What did Kurugu and Ameyaw find while hunting?

    A. A treasure chest

    B. A spider

    C. A rare flower

    D. A secret passage

47. What is the main idea of the passage?

    A. The discovery of a unique spider web technique

    B. The importance of hunting in the Ashanti Kingdom

    C. The role of women in weaving traditional fabrics

    D. The history and significance of Kente cloth

48. What does the word "interwoven" mean in the context of the passage?

    A. To tear apart

    B. To sew together

    C. To mix colors

    D. To cut into strips

49. Who used to wear Kente cloth during special occasions? *(Picture based question)*

    A. Picture of Men and women

    B. Picture of Children and elders

    C. Picture of Kings

    D. Picture of Holy animals

50. What does the word "mechanics" mean in the context of the passage?

    A. People who repair machines

    B. The study of motion and forces

    C. Tools and equipment used for weaving

    D. The detailed workings or processes

www.math-knots.com | www.a4ace.com

Grade 3
ELA Practice Test 2

Directions: *Read the passages and answer the questions that follow.*

YOUNG GEORGE AND THE COLT –

BY HORACE SCUDDER

There is a story told of George Washington's boyhood, —unfortunately there are not many stories, —which is to the point. His father had taken a great deal of pride in his blooded horses, and his mother afterward took pains to keep the stock pure. She had several young horses that had not yet been broken, and one of them in particular, a sorrel, was extremely spirited. No one had been able to do anything with it, and it was pronounced thoroughly vicious as people are apt to pronounce horses which they have not learned to master.

George was determined to ride this colt and told his companions that if they would help him catch it, he would ride and tame it.

Early in the morning they set out for the pasture, where the boys managed to surround the sorrel, and then to put a bit into its mouth. Washington sprang upon its back, the boys dropped the bridle, and away flew the angry animal.

Its rider at once began to command. The horse resisted, backing about the field, rearing and plunging. The boys became thoroughly alarmed, but Washington kept his seat, never once losing his self-control or his mastery of the colt.

The struggle was a sharp one; when suddenly, as if determined to rid itself of its rider, the creature leaped into the air with a tremendous bound. It was its last. The violence burst a blood-vessel, and the noble horse fell dead.

Before the boys could sufficiently recover to consider how they should extricate themselves from the scrape, they were called to breakfast; and the mistress of the house, knowing that they had been in the fields, began to ask after her stock.

"Pray, young gentlemen," said she, "have you seen my blooded colts in your rambles? I hope they are well taken care of. My favorite, I am told, is as large as his sire."

The boys looked at one another, and no one liked to speak. Of course, the mother repeated her question.

"The sorrel is dead, madam," said her son, "I killed him."

And then he told the whole story. They say that his mother flushed with anger, as her son often used to, and then, like him, controlled herself, and presently said, quietly: —

"It is well; but while I regret the loss of my favorite, I rejoice in my son who always speaks the truth."

1. What was the color of the young horse George Washington wanted to ride?

A) Bay
B) Sorrel
C) Chestnut
D) Black

2. Why did George Washington's mother keep the stock of horses pure?

A) To win horse racing competitions

B) To sell them at a higher price

C) To maintain their bloodline

D) To prevent them from classified as vicious

3. How did George Washington manage to ride the spirited colt?

    A) He used a lasso to catch it.

    B) His friends distracted the colt while he mounted it.

    C) He bribed the colt with treats.

    D) He trained the colt using a gentle approach.

4. What happened to the colt during George Washington's attempt to tame it?

    A) It threw him off and escaped.

    B) It surrendered and became docile.

    C) It fell ill and needed medical attention.

    D) It died from a burst blood vessel.

5. Why did the boys hesitate to speak when George Washington's mother asked about her colts?

    A) They were afraid of getting in trouble.

    B) They didn't want to upset her.

    C) They were still recovering from their scare.

    D) They were unsure of the fate of the other colts.

6. What quality did George Washington's mother admire in her son despite the loss of her favorite colt?

    A) His riding skills

    B) His ability to control the colt

    C) His truthfulness and honesty

    D) His determination to tame the colt

7. Which sentence best describes the spirited sorrel colt that George Washington wanted to ride?

    A) A lively, untamed horse with a fiery expression and lifted hooves.

    B) A calm, gentle horse peacefully grazing in a pasture.

    C) A tired, exhausted horse resting in a stable.

    D) A horse being trained and ridden by a professional equestrian.

8. Which sentence depicts the final moment of the colt's struggle

with George Washington?

A) George Washington firmly seated on the colt while it rears up in defiance.

B) The colt successfully throwing off George Washington and galloping away.

C) George Washington and the colt peacefully standing side by side after taming.

D) The colt lying lifeless on the ground after a burst blood vessel.

THE STORY OF THE INKY BOYS - HEINRICH HOFFMANN

As he had often done before,

The woolly-headed Black-a-moor

One nice fine summer's day went out

To see the shops, and walk about;

And, as he found it hot, poor fellow,

He took with him his green umbrella,

Then Edward, little noisy wag,

Ran out and laughed, and waved his flag;

And William came in jacket trim,

And brought his wooden hoop with him;

And Arthur, too, snatched up his toys

And joined the other naughty boys.

So, one and all set up a roar,

And laughed and hooted more and more,

And kept on singing, —only think! —

"Oh, Blacky, you're as black as ink!"

9. What did the Black-a-moor take with him on his outing?

    A) His black umbrella

    B) His green umbrella

    C) His wooden hoop

    D) His jacket

10. Who joined Edward in waving a flag?

    A) Arthur   B) William

    C) The Black-a-moor   D) No one

11. What did William bring with him?

    A) His wooden hoop   B) His green umbrella

    C) His jacket   D) His toys

12. How did the other boys react to the Black-a-moor?

    A) They laughed and hooted

    B) They sang a song

    C) They waved their flags

    D) They joined him for a walk

13. What did the boys tease the Black-a-moor about?

    A) His toys   B) His flag

    C) His black color   D) His umbrella

14. How did the Black-a-moor feel about the teasing?

    A) He ignored it

    B) He joined in the laughter

    C) He waved his flag in response

    D) His feelings were not mentioned

15. What was the weather like on the day the Black-a-moor went out?

    A) Rainy   B) Snowy

    C) Hot   D) Windy

       28   www.math-knots.com | www.a4ace.com

16. What color was the Black-a-moor?

A) Black as ink

B) Green

C) Woolly-headed

D) Not mentioned

THE BLUE BIRD – BY MAURICE-MAETERLINCK
AND GEORGETTE-LEBLANC

Now, one evening which was not like other evenings, for it was Christmas Eve, Mummy Tyl put her little ones to bed and kissed them even more lovingly than usual. She felt a little sad because, owing to the stormy weather, Daddy Tyl was not able to go to work in the forest; and so she had no money to buy presents with which to fill Tyltyl and Mytyl's stockings. The Children soon fell asleep, everything was still and silent and not a sound was heard but the purring of the cat, the snoring of the dog and the ticking of the great grandfather's clock. But suddenly a light as bright as day crept through the shutters, the lamp upon the table lit again of itself and the two Children awoke, yawned, rubbed their eyes, stretched out their arms in bed and Tyltyl, in a cautious voice called:

"Mytyl?"
"Yes, Tyltyl?" was the answer.
"Are you asleep?"
"Are you?"
"No," said Tyltyl. "How can I be asleep, when I'm talking to you?"
"I say, is this Christmas Day?" asked his sister.
"Not yet; not till tomorrow. But Father Christmas won't bring us anything this year."
"Why not?"
"I heard Mummy say that she couldn't go to town to tell him. But he will come next year."
"Is next year far off?"
"A good long while," said the boy. "But he will come to the rich children tonight."
"Really?"
"Hullo!" cried Tyltyl of a sudden. "Mummy's forgotten to put out the lamp! … I've an idea!"
"What?"
"Let's get up."
"But we mustn't," said Mytyl, who always remembered.
"Why, there's no one about! … Do you see the shutters?"
"Oh, how bright they are! …"
"It's the lights of the party," said Tyltyl.
"What party?"
"The rich children opposite. It's the Christmas-tree. Let's open the shutters. …"

www.math-knots.com | www.a4ace.com

17. Why did Mummy Tyl feel a little sad on Christmas Eve?

A) The children were misbehaving

B) Daddy Tyl could not go to work in the forest

C) The weather was stormy

D) The children were not asleep

18. What sound was NOT heard in the room as the children fell asleep?

A) Purring of the cat

B) Snoring of the dog

C) Ticking of the great-grandfather's clock

D) Laughter of the children

19. Read the dictionary entry:

arm [ahrm]

1. a sleeve of a garment.

2. each of the upper two limbs

3. used to refer to something powerful or protective

4. a side part of a chair

Which meaning of the word *arm* is used in the sentence –

the two Children awoke, yawned, rubbed their eyes, stretched out their arms in bed?

A) 1   B) 2

C) 3   D) 4

20. What woke up the two children in the middle of the night?

A) A bright light creeping through the shutters

B) A loud noise from outside

C) Mummy Tyl calling them

D) Father Christmas entering the room

www.math-knots.com | www.a4ace.com

21. **How did Tyltyl know that Father Christmas wouldn't bring them anything that year?**

    A) He overheard his parents talking

    B) The shutters were closed

    C) His sister told him

    D) He saw the lights of the party at the rich children's house

22. **Why did Tyltyl want to get up and open the shutters?**

    A) To see if it was Christmas Day

    B) To turn off the lamp

    C) To look for Father Christmas

    D) To see the Christmas tree at the party

23. **Why did Mytyl hesitate to get up?**

    A) She was afraid of the dark

    B) She thought they shouldn't get out of bed

    C) She was waiting for Father Christmas

    D) She wanted to play with the rich children

24. **What did Tyltyl think the bright lights were from?**

    A) The Christmas tree at the party

    B) The moon shining through the shutters

    C) Fireworks outside

    D) Mummy Tyl's candles

25. **What did Tyltyl and Mytyl expect to see when they opened the shutters?**

    A) Father Christmas delivering presents

    B) A snowy landscape

    C) The rich children playing with their gifts

    D) Mummy Tyl lighting candles

26. Which phrase represents the bright light creeping through the shutters that woke up the children?

A) A sun shining brightly in the sky

B) Moonlight casting a glow on the trees

C) A lamp turned on in a dark room

D) Sunlight filtering through closed shutters

27. Which description represents the scene described when the children saw the lights of the party at the rich children's house?

A) Children opening presents under a Christmas tree

B) Children dancing and playing at a birthday party

C) Brightly lit house with decorations and a Christmas tree

D) Children sleeping peacefully in their beds.

SUBMARINES: EXPLORING THE DEEP SEA

Submarines are amazing underwater vehicles that can explore the depths of the oceans. They are like special boats that can travel underwater, just like fish! Let's learn more about submarines.

1. A submarine is a big, strong ship designed to go underwater. It has a long and narrow shape, almost like a tube. The top part of a submarine, called the hull, is made of strong metal. This helps to keep the water out and keeps everyone inside safe and dry. Submarines also have a periscope, which is like a long telescope that sticks out of the water and allows the people inside to see what's happening above.

2. But how do submarines move underwater? Well, they have big propellers at the back, just like the ones on a boat. These propellers spin around, pushing the water backward and making the submarine move forward. Some submarines can go very fast, just like a speedy fish!

3. Inside a submarine, there are different sections or rooms. There is a control room where the captain and crew steer the submarine and make sure everything is working properly. There are also bedrooms for the crew to rest, a kitchen to prepare food, and even a place to exercise. Living in a submarine can be like living in a small, cozy home.

4. One very important thing about submarines is that they can go deep underwater, where it's very dark and cold. They have special equipment and lights to help the crew see and explore the mysterious ocean world. Submarines can even stay underwater for a long time, carrying supplies and equipment for scientific research or military missions.

5. In conclusion, submarines are fascinating machines that can explore the deep sea. They are like underwater boats with propellers and periscopes. They can go deep underwater, carry people, and stay underwater for a long time. Exploring the oceans in a submarine is like embarking on a thrilling adventure to discover the secrets hidden beneath the waves.

28. In which paragraph is the importance of lights and special equipment in submarines mentioned?

A) Paragraph 1

B) Paragraph 2

C) Paragraph 4

D) Paragraph 5

29. What is the top part of a submarine called?

A) Propeller

B) Periscope

C) Hull

D) Telescope

30. How do submarines move underwater?

A) By flapping their fins

B) By pedaling like a bicycle

C) By spinning propellers

D) By using oars

31. Which section of a submarine is responsible for steering and monitoring?

A) Control room

B) Kitchen

C) Bedroom

D) Exercise room

32. What is one special feature that helps the crew see in the dark underwater?

A) Periscope

B) Telescope

C) Propeller

D) Lights

33. What is the purpose of a periscope on a submarine?

A) To keep the water out

B) To carry supplies

C) To steer the submarine

D) To see above the water surface

34. What makes living in a submarine similar to living in a home?

A) Having a control room

B) Having a periscope

C) Having bedrooms

D) Having propellers

35. Where can submarines explore with their special equipment and lights?

A) Mountains

B) Deserts

C) Oceans

D) Forests

36. What can submarines carry for scientific research or military missions?

A) Food and water

B) Animals and plants

C) Supplies and equipment

D) Passengers and tourists

THE TALE OF SQUIRREL NUTKIN – BY BEATRIX POTTER

1. This is a Tale about a tail—a tail that belonged to a little red squirrel, and his name was Nutkin.

2. He had a brother called Twinkleberry, and a great many cousins: they lived in a wood at the edge of a lake.

3. In the middle of the lake there is an island covered with trees and nut bushes; and amongst those trees stands a hollow oak-tree, which is the house of an owl who is called Old Brown.

4. One autumn when the nuts were ripe, and the leaves on the hazel bushes were golden and green—Nutkin and Twinkleberry and all the other little squirrels came out of the wood, and down to the edge of the lake.

5. They made little rafts out of twigs, and they paddled away over the water to Owl Island to gather nuts.

6. Each squirrel had a little sack and a large oar, and spread out his tail for a sail.

7. They also took with them an offering of three fat mice as a present for Old Brown, and put them down upon his doorstep.

8. Then Twinkleberry and the other little squirrels each made a low bow, and said politely—

"Old Mr. Brown, will you flavour us with permission to gather nuts upon your island?"

9. But Nutkin was excessively impertinent in his manners. He bobbed up and down like a little red cherry, singing—

"Riddle me, riddle me, rot-tot-tote! A little wee man, in a red coat! A staff in his hand, and a stone in his throat; If you'll tell me this riddle, I'll give you a groat."

10. Now this riddle is as old as the hills; Mr. Brown paid no attention whatever to Nutkin.

11. He shut his eyes obstinately and went to sleep.

The squirrels filled their little sacks with nuts, and sailed away home in the evening.

12. But next morning they all came back again to Owl Island; and Twinkleberry and the others brought a fine fat mole, and laid it on the stone in front of Old Brown's doorway, and said—

"Mr. Brown, will you favor us with your gracious permission to gather some more nuts?"

37. In which paragraph is Nutkin introduced as a character?

A) Paragraph 1

B) Paragraph 2

C) Paragraph 3

D) Paragraph 4

38. What was the name of Nutkin's brother?

    A) Twinkleberry   B) Old Brown

    C) Nutkin   D) Mr. Brown

39. What did the squirrels use to make rafts?

    A) Leaves   B) Sticks

    C) Rocks   D) Feathers

40. How did Nutkin behave towards Old Brown?

    A) Respectfully   B) Impertinently

    C) Shyly   D) Gratefully

41. What did the squirrels bring to Old Brown the second time?

    A) Nuts   B) Mice

    C) Moles   D) Acorns

42. Which paragraph describes the squirrels' activity of making rafts

    and gathering nuts?

    A) Paragraph 4   B) Paragraph 5

    C) Paragraph 6   D) Paragraph 7

43. Read the sentence:

    Twinkleberry and the others brought a fine fat mole.

    Which meaning of the word 'fine' has been used in the sentence?

    A) very thin or narrow

    B) very good of its kind

    C) a sum of money to be paid as money

    D) made of small particles.

          www.math-knots.com | www.a4ace.com

IKTOMI AND THE DUCKS – ZITKALA-SA

1. Iktomi is a spider fairy. He wears brown deerskin leggins with long soft fringes on either side, and tiny beaded moccasins on his feet. His long black hair is parted in the middle and wrapped with red, red bands. Each round braid hangs over a small brown ear and falls forward over his shoulders.

2. He even paints his funny face with red and yellow, and draws big black rings around his eyes. He wears a deerskin jacket, with bright colored beads sewed tightly on it. Iktomi dresses like a real Dakota brave. In truth, his paint and deerskins are the best part of him—if ever dress is part of man or fairy.

3. Iktomi is a wily fellow. His hands are always kept in mischief. He prefers to spread a snare rather than to earn the smallest thing with honest hunting. Why! he laughs outright with wide open mouth when some simple folk are caught in a trap, sure and fast.

4. He never dreams another lives so bright as he. Often his own conceit leads him hard against the common sense of simpler people.

5. Poor Iktomi cannot help being a little imp. And so long as he is a naughty fairy, he cannot find a single friend. No one helps him when he is in trouble. No one really loves him. Those who come to admire his handsome beaded jacket and long fringed leggins soon go away sick and tired of his vain, vain words and heartless laughter.

6. Thus Iktomi lives alone in a cone-shaped wigwam upon the plain. One day he sat hungry within his teepee. Suddenly he rushed out, dragging after him his blanket. Quickly spreading it on the ground, he tore up dry tall grass with both his hands and tossed it fast into the blanket.

44. In which paragraph is Iktomi's appearance described?

    A) Paragraph 1   B) Paragraph 2

    C) Paragraph 3   D) Paragraph 4

45. According to the passage, what does Iktomi prefer to do?

    A) Earn things with honest hunting   B) Help others in need

    C) Spread traps and snares   D) Laugh with wide open mouth

46. Why does no one help Iktomi when he is in trouble?

    A) Because he has no friends

    B) Because he is a naughty fairy

    C) Because he is too conceited

    D) Because he lives alone in a wigwam

47. What do people think of Iktomi's vanity and heartless laughter?

A) They admire it

B) They find it amusing

C) They grow sick and tired of it

D) They try to imitate it

48. Why does Iktomi live alone in a cone-shaped wigwam?

A) Because he enjoys solitude

B) Because he doesn't like people

C) Because he has no friends

D) Because he prefers the wigwam over other homes

49. Based on the passage, what can you infer about Iktomi's behavior

and its effect on others?

A) Iktomi's behavior makes people admire him.

B) Iktomi's behavior causes people to avoid him.

C) Iktomi's behavior makes people want to imitate him.

D) Iktomi's behavior has no effect on others.

50. Which word rhymes with "moccasins"?

A) Deerskin   B) Mischief

C) Parted   D) Basins

Directions: *Read the passages and answer the questions that follow.*

THE OWL AND THE GRASSHOPPER

The Owl always takes her sleep during the day. Then after sundown, when the rosy light fades from the sky and the shadows rise slowly through the wood, out she comes ruffling and blinking from the old hollow tree. Now her weird "hoo-hoo-hoo-oo-oo" echoes through the quiet wood, and she begins her hunt for the bugs and beetles, frogs and mice she likes so well to eat.

Now there was a certain old Owl who had become very cross and hard to please as she grew older, especially if anything disturbed her daily slumbers. One warm summer afternoon as she dozed away in her den in the old oak tree, a Grasshopper nearby began a joyous but very raspy song. Out popped the old Owl's head from the opening in the tree that served her both for door and for window.

"Get away from here, sir," she said to the Grasshopper. "Have you no manners? You should at least respect my age and leave me to sleep in quiet!"

But the Grasshopper answered saucily that he had as much right to his place in the sun as the Owl had to her place in the old oak. Then he struck up a louder and still more rasping tune.

The wise old Owl knew quite well that it would do no good to argue with the Grasshopper, nor with anybody else for that matter. Besides, her eyes were not sharp enough by day to permit her to punish the Grasshopper as he deserved. So, she laid aside all hard words and spoke very kindly to him.

"Well sir," she said, "if I must stay awake, I am going to settle right down to enjoy your singing. Now that I think of it, I have a wonderful wine here, sent me from Olympus, of which I am told Apollo drinks before he sings to the high gods. Please come up and taste this delicious drink with me. I know it will make you sing like Apollo himself."

The foolish Grasshopper was taken in by the Owl's flattering words. Up he jumped to the Owl's den, but as soon as he was near enough so the old Owl could see him clearly, she pounced upon him and ate him up.

Flattery is not a proof of true admiration.

Do not let flattery throw you off your guard against an enemy.

1. **Owls hunt for—**
    A. Bugs
    B. Bugs and beetles
    C. Frogs and mice
    D. b and c

2. **"Get away from here sir"— who said this line?**
    A. Grasshopper
    B. Frog
    C. Old owl
    D. None of them

3. **The wonderful wine was sent from**
   A. Apollo
   B. A friend
   C. Olympus
   D. Jupiter

4. **Why did the owl call the grasshopper to her den?**
   A. To offer him a drink
   B. To teach him lesson
   C. To enjoy his singing
   D. To have company

5. **Why did the old owl become Cross and hard?**
   A. Because she had grown old
   B. Someone disturbed her slumber
   C. She couldn't see clearly
   D. A and B

6. **What does 'slumber' mean?**
   A. Reading
   B. Roar
   C. Sleep
   D. Hunt

7. **Which of the following is a synonym of saucily?**
   A. Impudently
   B. Humbly
   C. Modestly
   D. Politely

8. **Which of the following best describes the moral of the story?**
   A. All that glitters is not gold
   B. Flattery is not a proof of true admiration
   C. Don't let your enemy's flattery catch you unaware
   D. All of the above

                   www.math-knots.com | www.a4ace.com

OLD SULTAN

A shepherd had a faithful dog, called Sultan, who was grown very old, and had lost all his teeth. And one day when the shepherd and his wife were standing together before the house the shepherd said, 'I will shoot old Sultan tomorrow morning, for he is of no use now.' But his wife said, 'Pray let the poor faithful creature live; he has served us well a great many years, and we ought to give him a livelihood for the rest of his days.' 'But what can we do with him?' said the shepherd, 'he has not a tooth in his head, and the thieves don't care for him at all; to be sure he has served us, but then he did it to earn his livelihood; tomorrow shall be his last day, depend upon it.'

Poor Sultan, who was lying close by them, heard all that the shepherd and his wife said to one another, and was very much frightened to think tomorrow would be his last day; so in the evening, he went to his good friend the wolf, who lived in the wood, and told him all his sorrows, and how his master meant to kill him in the morning. 'Make yourself easy,' said the wolf, 'I will give you some good advice. Your master, you know, goes out every morning very early with his wife into the field; and they take their little child with them, and lay it down behind the hedge in the shade while they are at work. Now do you lie down close by the child, and pretend to be watching it, and I will come out of the wood and run away with it; you must run after me as fast as you can, and I will let it drop; then you may carry it back, and they will think you have saved their child and will be so thankful to you that they will take care of you as long as you live.' The dog liked this plan very well, and accordingly, it was managed. The wolf ran with the child a little way; the shepherd and his wife screamed out; but Sultan soon overtook him, and carried the poor little thing back to his master and mistress. Then the shepherd patted him on the head, and said, 'Old Sultan has saved our child from the wolf, and therefore he shall live and be well taken care of, and have plenty to eat. Wife, go home, give him a good dinner, and let him have my old cushion to sleep on as long as he lives.' So from this time forward, Sultan had all that he could wish for.

Soon afterwards the wolf came and wished him joy, and said, 'Now, my good fellow, you must tell no tales, but turn your head the other way when I want to taste one of the old shepherd's fine fat sheep.' 'No,' said the Sultan; 'I will be true to my master.' However, the wolf thought he was in a joke, and came one night to get a dainty morsel. But Sultan had told his master what the wolf meant to do; so he laid wait for him behind the barn door, and when the wolf was busy looking out for a good fat sheep, he had a stout cudgel laid about his back, that combed his locks for him finely.

Then the wolf was very angry, and called Sultan 'an old rogue,' and swore he would have his revenge. So the next morning the wolf sent the boar to challenge Sultan to come into the wood to fight the matter. Now Sultan had nobody he could ask to be his second but the shepherd's old three-legged cat; so he took her with him, and as the poor thing limped along with some trouble, she stuck up her tail straight in the air.

The wolf and the wild boar were first on the ground; and when they espied their enemies coming, and saw the cat's long tail standing straight in the air, they thought she was carrying a sword for Sultan to fight with; and every time she limped, they thought she was picking up a stone to throw at them; so they said they should not like this way of fighting, and the boar lay down behind a bush, and the wolf jumped up into a tree. Sultan and the cat soon came up, and looked about and wondered that no one was there. The boar, however, had not quite hidden himself, for his ears stuck out of the bush; and when he shook one of them a little, the cat, seeing something move, and thinking it was a mouse, sprang upon it, and bit and scratched it, so that the boar jumped up and grunted, and ran away, roaring out, 'Look up in the tree, there sits the one

www.math-knots.com | www.a4ace.com

who is to blame.' So they looked up, and espied the wolf sitting amongst the branches; and they called him a cowardly rascal, and would not suffer him to come down till he was heartily ashamed of himself, and had promised to be good friends again with old Sultan.

9. **What is the main concern for Sultan in the story?**
   A. Finding a new home
   B. Losing his teeth
   C. Becoming friends with the wolf
   D. Being killed by the shepherd

10. **Why does Sultan have to pretend to watch the sheep's child?**
   A. To fool the shepherd and his wife
   B. To earn a livelihood
   C. To play a game with the wolf
   D. To protect the child from danger

11. **What happens to the wolf when he tries to get a sheep from the shepherd's farm?**
   A. He gets hit with a cudgel
   B. He becomes friends with Sultan
   C. He escapes from Sultan
   D. He successfully steals a sheep

12. **Why does the cat have to limp?**
   A. Because it is following Sultan's lead
   B. Because it is a three-legged cat
   C. Because it is laughing at the situation
   D. Because it is injured during the fight

13. **Why do the wolf and the wild boar hide from Sultan and the cat?**
   A. They want to surprise Sultan and the cat
   B. They are waiting for a better opportunity to attack
   C. They mistake the cat's tail and limping for weapons
   D. They are afraid of Sultan's barking

14. **What does the boar reveal when the cat attacks its ear?**
   A. Its plan to become friends with the cat
   B. Its intention to attack Sultan
   C. The wolf's location
   D. Its secret hiding spot

15. **What characteristics of Sultan are most valued by the shepherd and his wife?**
   A. Physical strength and speed
   B. Intelligence and cleverness
   C. Good looks and charm
   D. Faithfulness and loyalty

www.math-knots.com | www.a4ace.com

16. Why does Sultan refuse to help the wolf steal from the shepherd's flock?
   A. He is loyal to his master
   B. He doesn't like the taste of sheep
   C. He is confused about the wolf's plan
   D. He thinks it's unfair to steal

17. Why does the wolf call Sultan 'an old rogue'?
   A. Because Sultan is very old
   B. Because Sultan foiled the wolf's plan
   C. Because Sultan betrayed his trust
   D. Because Sultan was mean to the wolf

THE QUARREL OF THE QUAILS

Once upon a time many quails lived together in a forest. The wisest of them all was their leader.

A man lived near the forest and earned his living by catching quails and selling them. Day after day he listened to the note of the leader calling the quails. By and by this man, the fowler, was able to call the quails together. Hearing the note the quails thought it was their leader who called.

When they were crowded together, the fowler threw his net over them and off he went into the town, where he soon sold all the quails that he had caught.

The wise leader saw the plan of the Fowler for catching the quails. He called the birds to him and said, "This fowler is carrying away so many of us, we must put a stop to it. I have thought of a plan; it is this: The next time the Fowler throws a net over you, each of you must put your head through one of the little holes in the net. Then all of you together must fly away to the nearest thorn bush. You can leave the net on the thorn bush and be free yourselves."

The quails said that was a very good plan and they would try it the next time the Fowler threw the net over them.

The very next day the fowler came and called them together. Then he threw the net over them. The quails lifted the net and flew away with it to the **nearest** thorn bush where they left it. They flew back to their leader to tell him how well his plan had worked.

The fowler was busy until evening getting his net off the thorns and he went home empty-handed. The next day the same thing happened, and the next. His wife was angry because he did not bring home any money, but the fowler said, "The fact is those quails are working together now. The moment my net is over them, off they fly with it, leaving it on a thorn bush. As soon as the quails begin to quarrel I shall be able to catch them."

Not long after this, one of the quails in **alighting** on their feeding ground, trod by accident on another's head. "Who trod on my head?" angrily cried the second. "I did, but I didn't mean to. Don't be angry," said the first quail, but the second quail was angry and said mean things.

45

Soon all the quails had taken sides in this quarrel. When the fowler came that day he flung his net over them, and this time instead of flying off with it, one side said, "Now, you lift the net," and the other side said, "Lift it yourself."

"You try to make us lift it all," said the quails on one side. "No, we don't!" said the others, "you begin and we will help," but neither side began.

So, the quails quarrelled, and while they were quarrelling the fowler caught them all in his net. He took them to town and sold them for a good price.

18. **Who was the wisest of all the quails in the forest?**
    A. The fowler
    B. The smallest of the quails
    C. The quail with the longest wingspan
    D. Their leader

19. **How did the Fowler catch the quails?**
    A. By throwing a net over them
    B. By bribing them with food
    C. By chasing them with a stick
    D. By using a trap

20. **What was the plan suggested by the quail leader to avoid getting caught by the fowler?**
    A. Call for help from other forest animals
    B. Find a hiding spot and stay there
    C. Put their heads through the holes in the net and fly away with it
    D. Attack and scare the Fowler away

21. **What did the quails do with the net after flying away with it?**
    A. Buried it underground
    B. Used it to catch other animals
    C. Carried it back to their nests
    D. Left it on a thorn-bush

22. **How did the quails react when the Fowler threw the net over them while they were quarrelling?**
    A. They started fighting with each other
    B. They flew away immediately
    C. They couldn't decide who should lift the net
    D. They kept their heads outside the net

23. **Why did the Fowler say the quails were easy to catch after they started arguing?**
    A. The net got entangled in the thorn-bush
    B. They were too busy quarrelling to fly away
    C. He could chase them more quickly now
    D. They had lost their ability to fly

24. Which of the following best explains the meaning of 'alighting' as
    used in the passage?
    A. descend from a train, bus, or other form of transport
    B. Being on fire
    C. Light up
    D. to descend from or as if from the air and come to rest

25. In which word does -est mean the same as it does in 'nearest'?

> The quails lifted the net and flew away with it to the **nearest**
>
> thorn-bush where they left it.

    A. Arrest
    B. Digest
    C. Farthest
    D. Quest

26. **What was the moral of the story?**
    A. Nice guys finish last
    B. Stick together and you'll succeed
    C. Unity is strength
    D. Don't trust anyone

CASABIANCA

There was a great battle at sea. One could hear nothing but the roar of the big guns. The air was filled with black smoke. The water was strewn with broken masts and pieces of timber which the cannon balls had knocked from the ships. Many men had been killed, and many more had been wounded.

The flagship had taken fire. The flames were breaking out from below. The deck was all ablaze. The men who were left alive made haste to launch a small boat. They leapt into it and rowed swiftly away. Any other place was safer now than on board that burning ship. There was powder in the hold.

But the captain's son, young Ca-sa-bi-an´ca, still stood upon the deck. The flames were almost all around him now, but he would not stir from his post. His father had bidden him to stand there, and he had been taught always to obey. He trusted in his father's word and believed that when the right time came he would tell him to go.

He saw the men leap into the boat. He heard them call to him to come. He shook his head.

"When father bids me, I will go," he said.

And now the flames were leaping up the masts. The sails were all ablaze. The fire blew hot upon his cheek. It scorched his hair. It was before him, behind him, all around him.

"O father!" he cried, "may I not go now? The men have all left the ship. Is it not time that we too should leave it?"

He did not know that his father was lying in the burning cabin below, that a cannonball had struck him dead at the very beginning of the fight. He listened to hear his answer.

"Speak louder, father!" he cried. "I cannot hear what you say."

Above the roaring of the flames, above the crashing of the falling spars, above the booming of the guns, he fancied that his father's voice came faintly to him through the scorching air.

"I am here, father! Speak once again!" he gasped.

But what is that?

A great flash of light fills the air; clouds of smoke shoot quickly upward to the sky; and—

"Boom!"

Oh, what a terrific sound! Louder than thunder, louder than the roar of all the guns! The air quivers; the sea itself trembles; the sky is black.

The blazing ship is seen no more.

There was powder in the hold!

27. What was the condition of the air during the naval battle?
    A. The air was filled with black smoke.
    B. The air was calm and still.
    C. The air was filled with the sound of cannons.
    D. The air was fresh and clean.

28. What made staying on board the burning ship dangerous?
    A. The ship was sinking fast.
    B. The enemy ships were approaching.
    C. The flames were spreading rapidly.
    D. There was power in the hold.

29. Why did young Casabianca stay on the burning ship?
    A. He trusted in his father's word and believed he would be told to go.
    B. He was too afraid to move.
    C. He didn't notice the flames.
    D. He wanted to impress the other men.

30. Why couldn't Casabianca hear his father?
    A. He was too far away from his father.
    B. His father had been killed at the beginning of the fight.
    C. Casabianca had gone deaf from the noise of the battle.
    D. The fire was too loud.

31. **What did Casabianca think he heard?**
    A. The crew calling for reinforcements.
    B. The sound of cannons firing in bursts.
    C. The ship creaking under pressure.
    D. His father's voice faintly through the scorching air.

32. **What ultimately brought an end to Casabianca's story?**
    A. Casabianca jumping into the boat.
    B. An explosion of powder.
    C. The rescue team reaching the ship in time.
    D. The ship sinking into the depths of the sea.

33. **What happened to the blazing ship after the explosion?**
    A. It drifted away with the current.
    B. It sank slowly into the sea.
    C. It was no longer visible.
    D. It crashed into the enemy ships.

34. **What does the phrase, 'The sky is black.' most likely imply?**
    A. The clouds covered the sky completely.
    B. There was a lot of smoke in the air.
    C. The enemy ships blocked out the sunlight.
    D. Night has fallen.

ELECTRICITY

1. ELECTRICITY was a property but imperfectly understood by the ancients; indeed, it has been said, they were entirely unacquainted with it. But we propose, shortly, to show the extent to which we are informed their sphere of knowledge extended. This much cannot be denied, that they were acquainted with the electrical properties of amber, of which fact we are informed by Pliny.

2. Even before Pliny, however, as early as the days of Thalis, who lived near six hundred years anterior to the Roman historian, the Miletine philosophers ascribed the attractive power of the magnet and of amber to animation by a vital principle. Our word "electricity" appears to be derived from the name the Latins gave to amber, _electrum_. It is also evident that they were acquainted with the shock of the torpedo; although they were ignorant, as are the moderns, of the concealed cause of this effect.

3. It has been asserted that the ancients knew how to collect the electrical fire in the atmosphere; and it is also said, that it was in an experiment of this nature that Tullus Hostilius lost his life. Etymologists have carried us still farther back, and assert that it was from the electrical property in the heavens that Jove obtained his surname of Jupiter _Eliaus_. This, however, may be only conjectural.

4. The first discoveries made of sufficient importance to demand the appellation of "scientific" in the science of electricity, were effected by Dr. W. Gilbert, the result of which he gave the world, in the year 1660, in a book then published, entitled "De Magneto," and Dr. Gilbert was followed in his pursuits by that celebrated scientific character, the honourable and illustrious Boyle, and other men eminent for that species of information.

www.math-knots.com | www.a4ace.com

5. This science was successfully cultivated in the last century by many eminent philosophers, among whom we may mention Hawkesbee, Grey, Muschenbrook, Doctors Franklin and Priestly, Bishop Watson, Mr. Cavendish, and several other members of the Royal Society of England; whilst those worthy of the true philosophic character in France did not neglect its cultivation.

6. Many fatal accidents have resulted from experiments made by people ignorant of the science. On the 6th of August, 1753, at Petersburg, Professor Richmann lost his life by endeavouring to draw the electric fluid into his house.

7. Electricity, like many others of the arcana of nature, still retains almost as deeply shaded from human view as when its existence was first made known.

8. Nature appears to have certain secret operations, which are not yet, perhaps, to be revealed.

35. According to the text, where did the Latin word 'electricity' come from?
    A. Magnet   B. Amber
    C. Torpedo   D. Atmosphere

36. What ancient philosopher believed that the attractive power of the magnet and amber was due to animation by a vital principle?
    A. Pliny   B. Jove
    C. Thalis   D. Tullus Hostilius

37. Which of the following best explains the meaning of 'arcana' as used in the sentence below?

> Electricity, like many others of the **arcana** of nature, still retains almost as deeply shaded from human view as when its existence was first made known.

    A. mysterious or specialized knowledge, language, or information accessible or possessed only by the initiate
    B. either of the two groups of cards in a tarot pack
    C. Withhold
    D. A chest

38. Which of the following sentences does not show that experimenting with electricity can be life-threatening?
    A. "It was in an experiment of this nature that Tullus Hostilius lost his life."
    B. "Professor Richmann lost his life by endeavouring to draw the electric fluid into his house."
    C. "Many fatal accidents have resulted from experiments made by people ignorant of the science."
    D. "It has been asserted that the ancients knew how to collect the electrical fire in the atmosphere"

www.math-knots.com | www.a4ace.com

39. Consider the following meanings:

> 1. situated before or toward the front
> 2. situated near or toward the head or part most nearly corresponding to a head
> 3. coming before in time or development

These refer to which word from the passage?

A. Anterior

B. Conjectural

C. Appellation

D. Acquainted

40. Who were some of the eminent philosophers who cultivated the science of electricity in the last century?

A. Thalis, Pliny, Tullus Hostilius

B. Jove, Torpedo, Amber

C. Hawkesbee, Grey, Muschenbrook

D. Dr W. Gilbert, Dr Priestly, Bishop Watson

41. Which of the following questions is answered in the 4th Para?

A. When were the first discoveries related to electricity by Dr W. Gilbert?

B. What do we know about the discovery of electricity in antiquity?

C. What were the contributions of the scientists of the Royal Society?

D. How the Miletine philosophers ascribed the attractive power of the magnet?

42. Which organization did many eminent philosophers in England, such as Doctors Franklin, Priestly, and Mr Cavendish, belong to?

A. the Latins

B. Miletine philosophers

C. Royal Society of England

D. the French Society for Scientific Advancement

SHAZADPUR,

June 1891.

I had a most extraordinary dream last night. The whole of Calcutta seemed enveloped in some awful mystery, the houses being only dimly visible through a dense, dark mist, within the veil of which there were strange doings.

I was going along Park Street in a hackney carriage, and as I passed St. Xavier's College. I found it had started growing rapidly and was fast getting impossibly high within its enveloping haze. Then it was borne in on me that a band of magicians had come to Calcutta who, if they were paid for it, could bring about many such wonders.

When I arrived at our Jorasanko house, I found these magicians had turned up there too. They were ugly-looking, of a Mongolian type, with scanty moustaches and a few long hairs sticking out of their chins. They could make men grow. Some of the girls wanted to be made taller, and the magician sprinkled some powder over their heads and they promptly shot up. To everyone I met, I kept repeating: "This is most extraordinary, —just like a dream!"

   www.math-knots.com | www.a4ace.com

Then someone proposed that our house should be made to grow. The magicians agreed, and as a preliminary began to take down some portions. The dismantling over, they demanded money, or else they would not go on. The cashier strongly objected. How could payment be made before the work was completed? At this the magicians got wild and twisted up the building most fearsomely so that men and brickwork got mixed together, bodies inside walls and only head and shoulders showing.

It had altogether the look of a thoroughly devilish business, as I told my eldest brother. "You see," said I, "the kind of thing it is. We had better call upon God to help us!" But try as I might to curse them in the name of God, my heart felt like breaking and no words would come. Then I awoke.

A curious dream, was it not? Calcutta in the hands of Satan and growing diabolically, within the darkness of an unholy mist!

43. What enveloped the whole of Calcutta in the dream?

    A. heavy rain   B. thick fog

    C. dense, dark mist   D. bright sunlight

44. Where did Tagore see St. Xavier's College in the dream?

    A. Park Street   B. outside Calcutta

    C. Jorasanko house   D. At Shazadpur

45. What could the magicians do according to the dream?

    A. turn men into animals   B. make men shrink

    B. make men grow   D. make men invisible

46. What did the magician sprinkle over the heads of the girls?

    A. Powder   B. water

    C. Salt   D. oil

47. When seeing the magicians in the house, what did Tagore repeatedly say?

    A. "This is scary, I'm going home!"

    B. "What a coincidence!"

    C. "Am I hallucinating?"

    D. "This is most extraordinary, —just like a dream!"

48. Why did the magicians get wild during the dismantling of the house?

    A. because they thought they were being mistreated

    B. because the cashier strongly objected to paying before the work was completed

    C. because the magicians didn't know how to continue with the work

    D. because they wanted to keep the house for themselves

49. What did the dreamer suggest to his eldest brother in response to the magicians' actions?

    A. "We should fight them ourselves!"

    B. "Let's run away from this place!"

    C. "Maybe we should let them do what they want"

    D. "We had better call upon God to help us!"

50. What did the dreamer compare the appearance of the building and the people inside to?

    A. a funny circus act   B. a thoroughly devilish business

    C. a beautiful work of art   D. an engineering marvel

 www.math-knots.com | www.a4ace.com

Directions: *Read the passages and answer the questions that follow.*

Kaa's Hunting

Before Mowgli left the Free People, he was under the tutelage of Baloo and Bagheera. In this tale, they teach him the Law of the Jungle, which most wolf cubs don't learn fully. He learns how to speak to snakes, birds and other beasts, to hail them and to ask for permission not to be harmed by them.

One day after being cuffed by Baloo for not reciting the Law correctly, Mowgli leaves in a huff and plays with the Monkey People, the Bandar-log, and they tell him that someday he will be their leader. When Baloo learns about this, he becomes angry. The Jungle People ignore the Monkey People because of their foolishness.

Before long, the Monkey People kidnap Mowgli. They toss him between them as they travel to the Cold Lair, an Indian ruin in the Jungle. Mowgli hails a bird to tell Baloo and Bagheera where he's being taken. Baloo and Bagheera know the Bandar-log fears Kaa the Rock Python, so they find him and ask for help. All he knows is that the Bandar-log have changed their hunting grounds. Just then, a bird tells them that the Monkey People have taken Mowgli to the Cold Lairs. Meanwhile, Mowgli tries to leave the Cold Lairs, but the Monkey People pull him back and tell him why he wants to be with them and how amazing they are. When Bagheera arrives and attacks, over 100 monkeys attack him and throw Mowgli into an area filled with poisonous snakes. Mowgli speaks friendship to the snakes, and they agree not to bite him. When Baloo arrives, he begins to fight against the Bandar-log, too.

Then Kaa comes and the monkeys flee. Kaa's hissing and movement puts them in a trance. Kaa breaks the wall holding Mowgli, and then Baloo and Bagheera fall into the snake's trance, too. Mowgli thanks the python, snaps his friends out of their trance and leaves. The Law of the Jungle requires that Mowgli be cuffed for his mischievousness, but Bagheera cuffs him lightly, though it is quite a beating for a 7-year-old. Then they all head for their respective homes.

(ADAPTED FROM: THE JUNGLE BOOK, RUDYARD KIPLING)

1. What did Baloo and Bagheera teach Mowgli during his time with them?
   A. How to speak to wolves and other animals in the jungle.
   B. The Law of the Jungle and how to communicate with various creatures.
   C. The art of survival and hunting skills.
   D. How to lead the Free People and become their ruler.

2. Why did Baloo become angry when he learned that Mowgli had been playing with the Bandar-log?
   A. Because the Bandar-log were foolish and disliked by the Jungle People.
   B. Because Mowgli disobeyed him and went against the Law of the Jungle.
   C. Because the Bandar-log wanted Mowgli to become their leader.
   D. Because Mowgli was not reciting the Law correctly.

3. How did Mowgli manage to escape from the Cold Lair after being kidnapped by the Monkey People?

    A. He fought against the monkeys and managed to flee on his own.

    B. He called for help from Baloo and Bagheera using a bird as a messenger.

    C. He convinced the snakes in the area not to harm him.

    D. Kaa the Rock Python broke the wall holding him and helped him escape.

4. How did Kaa the Rock Python assist Mowgli, Baloo, and Bagheera in dealing with the Monkey People?

    A. Kaa attacked the Monkey People and drove them away.

    B. Kaa put the Monkey People in a trance, allowing Mowgli and his friends to escape.

    C. Kaa helped Mowgli convince the Monkey People to release him.

    D. Kaa provided valuable information about the Bandar-log's location.

5. Which of the following actions by Bagheera prove that he punished Mowgli for his mischievous activity?

    A. Bagheera cuffed Mowgli lightly, considering his young age.

    B. Bagheera gave Mowgli a severe beating as per the Law of the Jungle.

    C. Bagheera decided not to punish Mowgli for his mischievousness.

    D. Bagheera left the punishment to Baloo, the bear.

6. Which dictionary meaning of the word 'mischievous' (last paragraph) matches the context of the given passage?

> *1. behaving in a way, that is slightly bad*
>
> *2. causing trouble,*
>
> *3. deliberately causing harm or damage*
>
> *4. causing damage to somebody's reputation*

    A. 1

    B. 2

    C. 3

    D. 4

7. Which paragraph mentions Kaa putting the monkeys in a trance?

    A. Paragraph 1

    B. Paragraph 2

    C. Paragraph 3

    D. Paragraph 4

    56   www.math-knots.com | www.a4ace.com

The Bronze Ring

Once upon a time in a certain country there lived a king whose palace was surrounded by a spacious garden. But though the gardeners were many and the soil was good, this garden yielded neither flowers nor fruits, not even grass or shady trees.

The King was in despair about it, when a wise old man said to him:

"Your gardeners do not understand their business: but what can you expect of men whose fathers were cobblers and carpenters? How should they have learned to cultivate your garden?"

"You are quite right," cried the King.

"Therefore," continued the old man, "you should send for a gardener whose father and grandfather have been gardeners before him, and very soon your garden will be full of green grass and gay flowers, and you will enjoy its delicious fruit."

So, the King sent messengers to every town, village, and hamlet in his dominions, to look for a gardener whose forefathers had been gardeners also, and after forty days one was found.

"Come with us and be gardener to the King," they said to him.

"How can I go to the King," said the gardener, "a poor wretch like me?"

"That is of no consequence," they answered. "Here are new clothes for you and your family."

"But I owe money to several people."

"We will pay your debts," they said.

So, the gardener allowed himself to be persuaded, and went away with the messengers, taking his wife and his son with him; and the King, delighted to have found a real gardener, entrusted him with the care of his garden. The man found no difficulty in making the royal garden produce flowers and fruit, and at the end of a year the park was not like the same place, and the King showered gifts upon his new servant.

The gardener, as you have heard already, had a son, who was a very handsome young man, with most agreeable manners, and every day he carried the best fruit of the garden to the King, and all the prettiest flowers to his daughter. Now this princess was wonderfully pretty and was just sixteen years old, and the King was beginning to think it was time that she should be married.

"My dear child," said he, "you are of an age to take a husband; therefore, I am thinking of marrying you to the son of my prime minister.

"Father," replied the Princess, "I will never marry the son of the minister."

"Why not?" asked the King.

"Because I love the gardener's son," answered the Princess.

On hearing this the King was at first very angry, and then he wept and sighed, and declared that such a husband was not worthy of his daughter; but the young Princess was not to be turned from her resolution to marry the gardener's son.

Then the King consulted his ministers. "This is what you must do," they said. "To get rid of the gardener you must send both suitors to a very distant country, and the one who returns first shall marry your daughter."

The King followed this advice, and the minister's son was presented with a splendid horse and a purse full of gold pieces, while the gardener's son had only an old lame horse and a purse full of copper money, and everyone thought he would never come back from his journey.

(ADAPTED FROM: THE BLUE FAIRY BOOK, ANDREW LANG)

8. Why was the King's garden unproductive?

    A. The soil was poor

    B. The gardeners were lazy

    C. The gardeners lacked knowledge and experience

    D. The garden was cursed

9. What did the wise old man suggest to the King?

    A. To hire more gardeners

    B. To plant different types of seeds

    C. To bring in a skilled gardener with a family history of gardening

    D. To give up on the garden

10. "How can I go to the King?" The gardener says this and initially hesitate to go and work for the King because:

    A. He was afraid of the King's wrath

    B. He didn't want to leave his family

    C. He owed money to several people

    D. He didn't believe in his gardening abilities

11. How did the King convince the gardener to come and work for him?

    A. He promised to make him rich

    B. He threatened him with punishment if he refused

    C. He paid off the gardener's debts and offered new clothes

    D. He offered him the hand of the Princess in marriage

12. What was the result of the gardener's work in the royal garden?

    A. The garden remained unproductive

    B. The garden became full of green grass and flowers

    C. The garden turned into a dense forest

    D. The garden was destroyed by pests

13. Why did the King want to marry off his daughter?

    A. She was getting too old to be unmarried

    B. He wanted to form an alliance with another powerful family

    C. He wanted to get rid of her

    D. He wanted to see her settled and happy

14. Why did the King become angry when the Princess declared her love for the gardener's son?

    A. He didn't like the gardener's son

    B. He wanted her to marry the son of his prime minister

    C. He was worried about the gardener's social status

    D. He believed the gardener's son was not worthy of her

        www.math-knots.com | www.a4ace.com

15. The dictionary meanings of the word '*consequence*' are:

    1. Result or Outcome

    2. flow of events

    3. importance

    4. logical statement

The sentence where the word has been used in the passage: *"That is of no consequence," they answered.* *"Here are new clothes for you and your family."*

Which dictionary meaning of the word 'consequence' matches the context of the given passage:

    A. 1

    B. 2

    C. 3

    D. 4

16. What did the King hope to achieve by sending the two suitors to a distant country?

    A. He wanted to test their loyalty and determination.

    B. He wanted to see who could find the most valuable gifts.

    C. He wanted to determine who was the better gardener.

    D. He wanted to decide who was more suitable for his daughter.

The Life Cycle of a Butterfly

Butterflies are fascinating creatures that undergo a remarkable transformation during their life cycle. This process, known as metamorphosis, involves four distinct stages: egg, larva (caterpillar), pupa (chrysalis), and adult (butterfly). Let us explore each stage of their life cycle.

Stage 1: Egg The life cycle of a butterfly begins when the female butterfly lays tiny eggs on the leaves of specific plants. These eggs are often round or oval and may be attached individually or in clusters. The eggs are well-camouflaged to protect them from predators. Within a few days, the egg hatches, revealing a tiny caterpillar.

Stage 2: Larva (Caterpillar) The caterpillar is the second stage in a butterfly's life cycle. It is the feeding stage, and the caterpillar's primary goal is to eat and grow. Caterpillars have strong jaws, which they use to munch on leaves and plants. As they consume food, they grow rapidly and shed their skin multiple times to accommodate their increasing size. This process is called molting. Some caterpillars have fascinating patterns and colors, while others may have spines or hair for protection.

Stage 3: Pupa (Chrysalis) When the caterpillar has grown to its full size, it enters the third stage of its life cycle called the pupa or chrysalis. The caterpillar attaches itself to a surface using silk threads and sheds its outer skin one final time. Underneath this skin is the chrysalis, which may look like a delicate, suspended jewel. Inside the chrysalis, the caterpillar's body undergoes a remarkable transformation, breaking down into a soup-like substance and reforming into a butterfly.

 www.math-knots.com | www.a4ace.com

Stage 4: Adult (Butterfly) After a period of time, the chrysalis splits open, and a fully developed adult butterfly emerges. At first, the butterfly's wings are small, soft, and wrinkled. Th e butterfly must pump bodily fluids into its wings to expand them fully. Once the wings are fully expanded and dry, the butterfly is ready to take its first flight. Adult butterflies feed on nectar from flowers using their long proboscis, a tube - like structure that acts as a straw. Butterflies are essential pollinators, helping plants reproduce by transferring pollen from one flower to another.

17. What is the second stage in a butterfly's life cycle called?
- A. Pupa
- B. Egg
- C. Larva
- D. Adult

18. What is the primary goal of a caterpillar during its life cycle?
- A. To lay eggs
- B. To eat and grow
- C. To transform into a chrysalis
- D. To fly and collect nectar

19. Which stage of a butterfly's life cycle involves the transformation from a caterpillar into a butterfly?
- A. Egg
- B. Pupa (Chrysalis)
- C. Larva
- D. Adult

20. How do adult butterflies help plants reproduce?
- A. By laying eggs on plant leaves
- B. By shedding their skin
- C. By transferring pollen from one flower to another
- D. By forming a chrysalis

21. The word "camouflaged" is used to describe the appearance of butterfly eggs. What does "camouflaged" mean?
- A. Attractive and colorful
- B. Hidden or concealed from view
- C. Unusual or bizarre in appearance
- D. Laid in large clusters

22. What does the term "proboscis" refer to in the context of the passage?
- A. The long, tube-like structure used by adult butterflies to collect nectar from flowers
- B. The process of molting and shedding the caterpillar's skin
- C. The final stage of a butterfly's life cycle
- D. The delicate and suspended structure of the chrysalis

               www.math-knots.com | www.a4ace.com

23. **Which stage of a butterfly's life cycle involves the caterpillar shedding its outer skin multiple times to accommodate its increasing size?**
    A. Egg
    B. Larva (Caterpillar)
    C. Pupa (Chrysalis)
    D. Adult (Butterfly)

24. **Why are butterflies considered essential pollinators according to the Information in the passage?**
    A. They lay tiny eggs on the leaves of specific plants.
    B. They undergo a remarkable transformation during metamorphosis.
    C. They have strong jaws to munch on leaves and plants.
    D. They transfer pollen from one flower to another while feeding on nectar.

25. *The following are the dictionary meanings for the word 'splits' (Stage 4):*
    1. to break
    2. to end an emotional relationship
    3. to jump into the air and then sit with legs apart
    4. to suffer from headache

    Which dictionary meaning of the word '*splits*' matches the context of the given passage:
    A. 1
    B. 2
    C. 3
    D. 4

The Talking Bird, The Singing Tree, And The Golden Water

There was an emperor of Persia named Kosrouschah, who, when he first came to his crown, in order to obtain a knowledge of affairs, took great pleasure in night excursions, attended by a trusty minister. He often walked in disguise through the city, and met with many adventures, one of the most remarkable of which happened to him upon his first ramble, which was not long after his accession to the throne of his father.

After the ceremonies of his father's funeral rites and his own inauguration were over, the new sultan, as well from inclination as from duty, went out one evening attended by his grand vizier, disguised like himself, to observe what was transacting in the city. As he was passing through a street in that part of the town inhabited only by the meaner sort, he heard some people talking very loud; and going close to the house whence the noise proceeded, and looking through a crack in the door, perceived a light, and three sisters sitting on a sofa, conversing together after supper. By what the eldest said he presently understood the subject of their conversation was wishes: "for," said she, "since we are talking about wishes, mine shall be to have the sultan's baker for my husband, for then I shall eat my fill of that bread, which by way of excellence is called the sultan's; let us see if your tastes are as good as mine."

"For my part," replied the second sister, "I wish I was wife to the sultan's chief cook, for then I should eat of the most excellent dishes; and as I am persuaded that the sultan's bread is common in the palace, I should not want any of that; therefore you see," addressing herself to her eldest sister, "that I have a better taste than you." The youngest sister, who was very beautiful, and had more charms and wit than the two elder, spoke in her turn: "For my part, sisters," said she, "I shall not limit my desires to such trifles, but take a higher flight; and since we are upon wishing, I wish to be the emperor's queen-consort. I would make him father of a prince, whose hair should be gold on one side of his head, and silver on the other; when he cried, the tears from his eyes should be pearls; and when he smiled, his vermilion lips should look like a rosebud fresh-blown."

(ADAPTED FROM: THE ARABIAN NIGHTS)

26. Why did the emperor take night excursions through the city?
    A. To meet with his trusty minister
    B. To observe what was transacting in the city
    C. To attend his father's funeral rites
    D. To become the sultan's chief cook

27. What were the three sisters in the story discussing?
    A. Their favorite books
    B. Their wishes
    C. Their favorite foods
    D. Their travel plans

28. What did the eldest sister wish for?
    A. To be the emperor's queen-consort
    B. To eat the sultan's bread
    C. To become the sultan's baker's wife
    D. To eat the most excellent dishes

29. What did the youngest and most beautiful sister wish for?
   A. To be the emperor's queen-consort and have a special son
   B. To eat the sultan's bread
   C. To become the sultan's chief cook's wife
   D. To eat the most excellent dishes and have a special son

30. Which word in paragraph 2 signifies *a high-ranking officer*?
   A. subject
   B. vizier
   C. husband
   D. none of the above

31. What is the main reason Emperor Kosrouschah and his grand vizier disguise themselves and roam the city at night?
   A. To engage in adventures
   B. To observe the city's activities
   C. To escape from their duties
   D. To find suitable persons for important positions

32. Why does the youngest sister's wish stand out from the wishes of her two elder sisters?
   A. She wishes for a realistic outcome.
   B. She expresses a desire for riches.
   C. Her wish shows that she understands power.
   D. She wishes for something unimportant compared to her sisters.

33. The word *disguise* means to alter one's appearance.
   In which of the following sentences has the word been used *incorrectly*?
   A. The spy used a clever disguise to blend in with the crowd
   B. The disguise ran so fast that the police could not catch it.
   C. She wore a colourful mask as a disguise.
   D. The detective had to quickly come up with a new disguise to avoid being recognized by the criminal.

34. Which sister had the highest and most extravagant wish?
   A. The eldest sister
   B. The second sister
   C. The youngest sister
   D. All three had similar wishes

The Emperor's New Clothes

1. Many years ago, there was an Emperor, who was so excessively fond of new clothes, that he spent all his money in dress. He did not trouble himself in the least about his soldiers; nor did he care to go either to the theatre or the chase, except for the opportunities then afforded him for displaying his new clothes. He had a different suit for each hour of the day; and as of any other king or emperor, one is accustomed to say, "he is sitting in council," it was always said of him, "The Emperor is sitting in his wardrobe."

2. Time passed merrily in the large town which was his capital; strangers arrived every day at the court. One day, two rogues, calling themselves weavers, made their appearance. They gave out that they knew how to weave stuffs of the most beautiful colors and elaborate patterns, the clothes manufactured from which should have the wonderful property of remaining invisible to everyone who was unfit for the office he held, or who was extraordinarily simple in character.

3. "These must, indeed, be splendid clothes!" thought the Emperor. "Had I such a suit, I might at once find out what men in my realms are unfit for their office, and also be able to distinguish the wise from the foolish! This stuff must be woven for me immediately." And he caused large sums of money to be given to both the weavers in order that they might begin their work directly.

4. So the two pretended weavers set up two looms, and affected to work very busily, though in reality they did nothing at all. They asked for the most delicate silk and the purest gold thread; put both into their own knapsacks; and then continued their pretended work at the empty looms until late at night.

5. "I should like to know how the weavers are getting on with my cloth," said the Emperor to himself, after some little time had elapsed; he was, however, rather embarrassed, when he remembered that a simpleton, or one unfit for his office, would be unable to see the manufacture. To be sure, he thought he had nothing to risk in his own person; but yet, he would prefer sending somebody else, to bring him intelligence about the weavers, and their work, before he troubled himself in the affair. All the people thr oughout the city had heard of the wonderful property the cloth was to possess; and all were anxious to learn how wise, or how ignorant, their neighbors might prove to be.

6. "I will send my faithful old minister to the weavers," said the Emperor at last, after some deliberation, "he will be best able to see how the cloth looks; for he is a man of sense, and no one can be more suitable for his office than he is."

7. So the faithful old minister went into the hall, where the knaves were working with all their might, at their empty looms. "What can be the meaning of this?" thought the old man, opening his eyes very wide. "I cannot discover the least bit of thread on the looms." However, he did not express his thoughts aloud.

(Adapted From: Andersen's Fairy Tales, Hans Christian Andersen)

35. **What wonderful property did the clothes made by the weavers possess?**
    A. They were of the most beautiful colors and patterns.
    B. They were invisible to everyone.
    C. They could change colors.
    D. They were exceptionally warm.

36. **Why did the Emperor want the weavers to weave the cloth for him?**
    A. He wanted to sell the cloth to other kingdoms.
    B. He wanted to have different suits for every hour of the day.
    C. He wanted to distinguish wise people from foolish ones.
    D. He wanted to support the weavers financially.

37. **What did the weavers actually do when they pretended to work?**
    A. They wove intricate patterns with silk and gold thread.
    B. They worked diligently on the looms all day.
    C. They stored silk and gold thread in their knapsacks.
    D. They consulted with the Emperor about the designs.

38. **Why was the Emperor embarrassed about seeing the cloth himself?**
    A. He feared that he might not be able to afford the cloth.
    B. He worried that he might be considered a simpleton.
    C. He didn't want to interrupt the weavers' work.
    D. He preferred sending someone else to get the information.

39. **The word 'deliberation' in paragraph 6, in this context defines which of the following?**
    A. the quality or state of being deliberate
    B. a discussion and consideration by a group of people
    C. the act of thinking about something or discussing something and deciding carefully
    D. none of the above

40. **What did the old minister find when he went to see the weavers' work?**
    A. The weavers were working diligently on the looms.
    B. He couldn't see any cloth on the looms.
    C. The cloth was of the most beautiful colors and patterns.
    D. The weavers had finished their work and were packing up.

41. **In which paragraph does the Emperor express his fascination with new clothes and his disregard for other matters?**
    A. Paragraph 1
    B. Paragraph 2
    C. Paragraph 3
    D. Paragraph 4

42. Why does the Emperor decide to send his old minister to assess the weavers' work?

    A. He believes the minister is skilled at weaving.

    B. He wants the minister to learn the weaving technique.

    C. He thinks the minister is the wisest person in the city.

    D. He wishes to test the minister's loyalty and honesty.

The Little Mermaid

1. FAR out in the wide sea, —where the water is blue as the loveliest cornflower, and clear as the purest crystal, where it is so deep that very, very many church towers must be heaped one upon another in order to reach from the lowest depth to the surface above, —dwell the Mer-people.

2. Now you must not imagine that there is nothing but sand below the water: no, indeed, far from it! Trees and plants of wondrous beauty grow there, whose stems and leaves are so light, that they are waved to and fro by the slightest motion of the water, almost as if they were living beings. Fishes, great and small, glide in and out among the branches, just as birds fly about among our trees.

3. Where the water is deepest stands the palace of the Mer-king. The walls of this palace are of coral, and the high, pointed windows are of amber; the roof, however, is composed of mussel-shells, which, as the billows pass over them, are continually opening and shutting. This looks exceedingly pretty, especially as each of these mussel-shells contains a number of bright, glittering pearls, one only of which would be the most costly ornament in the diadem of a king in the upper world.

4. The Mer-king, who lived in this palace, had been for many years a widower; his old mother managed the household affairs for him. She was, on the whole, a sensible sort of a lady, although extremely proud of her high birth and station, on which account she wore twelve oysters on her tail, whilst the other inhabitants of the sea, even those of distinction, were allowed only six. In every other respect she merited unlimited praise, especially for the affection she showed to the six little princesses, her grand-daughters. These were all very beautiful children; the youngest was, however, the most lovely; her skin was as soft and delicate as a rose-leaf, her eyes were of as deep a blue as the sea, but like all other mermaids, she had no feet, her body ended in a tail like that of a fish.

5. The whole day long the children used to play in the spacious apartments of the palace, where beautiful flowers grew out of the walls on all sides around them. When the great amber windows were opened, fishes would swim into these apartments as swallows fly into our rooms; but the fishes were bolder than the swallows, they swam straight up to the little princesses, ate from their hands, and allowed themselves to be caressed.

6. In front of the palace there was a large garden, full of fiery red and dark blue trees, whose fruit glittered like gold, and whose flowers resembled a bright, burning sun. The sand that formed the soil of the garden was of a bright blue colour, something like flames of Sulphur; and a strangely beautiful blue was spread over the whole, so that one might have fancied oneself raised very high in the air, with the sky at once above and below, certainly not at the bottom of the sea. When the waters were quite still, the sun might be seen looking like a purple flower, out of whose cup streamed forth the light of the world.

(Adapted From: The Little Mermaid, Hans Christian Andersen)

43. What is unique about the youngest princess's body?
    A. She has wings like a bird.
    B. She has a fish tail instead of feet.
    C. She has arms made of coral.
    D. She has a magical wand.

44. What color is the sand in the garden in front of the palace?
    A. Fiery red and dark blue
    B. Glittering gold
    C. Bright blue like flames of Sulphur
    D. Deep green like seaweed

45. What did the fishes do when they entered the palace apartments?
    A. They flew around like birds.
    B. They ate fruits from the trees.
    C. They allowed themselves to be caressed by the princesses.
    D. They sang beautiful songs.

46. In which paragraph is the Mer-king's palace described, including details about its construction and ornaments?
    A. Paragraph 1
    B. Paragraph 2
    C. Paragraph 3
    D. Paragraph 4

47. Which paragraph provides a description of the garden in front of the palace, highlighting the unique and vibrant colors of the flora and the sand?
    A. Paragraph 4
    B. Paragraph 5
    C. Paragraph 6
    D. Paragraph 2

48. **Based on the passage, what can be inferred about the Mer-people's perception of beauty and aesthetics?**
   A. The Mer-people have a preference for dull and muted colors in their surroundings.
   B. The Mer-people appreciate the vivid and vibrant colors of nature, evident in their palace and garden.
   C. The Mer-people avoid decorating their surroundings and prefer a minimalistic lifestyle.
   D. The Mer-people dislike interacting with fishes and other underwater creatures due to their appearance.

49. **How does the description of the Mer-king's mother's appearance highlight her status and personality?**
   A. Her twelve oysters on her tail emphasize her modesty and humility.
   B. Her extravagant jewellery and attire showcase her wealth and opulence.
   C. Her lack of adornments signifies her desire for anonymity and privacy.
   D. Her six oysters on her tail symbolize her close relationship with her granddaughters.

50. **Identify the suffix in the word 'sensible'.**
   A. -ble
   B. -le
   C. -ible
   D. -sible

Grade 3
Answer Keys

Long the Dragon: Bringing Luck and Good Fortune

1. Answer: **C. Controlling water**

Explanation: Long, the dragon, had the special ability to control water. He could make it rain and bring water to the land, which was very helpful during a drought. This ability allowed him to help the farmers and make the crops grow again. The other choices, A) controlling the wind, B) making it snow, and D) controlling fire, are incorrect because the story specifically mentions Long's power to control water, not these other elements. The story tells us how Long used his powers to bring rain and help the people, making it clear that his special ability was controlling water, not wind, snow, or fire.

2. Answer: **B. Holy**

Explanation: In this passage, the word "divine" means holy. It describes Long, the dragon, as a creature who is considered sacred and connected to a higher power. The other choices, A) powerful, C) mythical, and D) helpful, are incorrect because they do not capture the meaning of the word "divine" as it is used in this passage. The passage tells us that Long, the dragon, was known as the most powerful and divine creature in China, emphasizing his holiness and significance.

3. Answer: **D. All of the above**

Explanation: The people of China were thankful to Long for multiple reasons. First, he made it rain when there was a terrible drought, which helped the crops grow again. This shows that choice B) "He made it rain" is correct. Additionally, Long was known as the symbol of good fortune, so he brought luck to the farmers' crops, as mentioned in choice C) "He brought good luck to their crops." Moreover, the story does not mention specifically about controlling the wind, so choice A) "He controlled the wind" is incorrect. However, since Long's actions of making it rain and bringing good luck to the crops were mentioned and appreciated by the people, the correct answer is D) "All of the above."

4. Answer: **C. They started to die**

Explanation: When the drought hit the land, the crops started to die. This means that choice C) "They started to die" is the correct answer. The story mentions that a terrible drought occurred, and the people started to worry because the crops were dying. This shows that the crops were not growing faster or getting bigger, as mentioned in choices A) "They grew faster" and B) "They got bigger." Additionally, there is no information in the story about the crops being moved to a different location, so choice D) "They were moved to a different location" is incorrect. Therefore, the correct answer is C) "They started to die" because the drought had a negative impact on the crops, causing them to wither and perish.

5. Answer: **B. Dry spell**

Explanation: In this passage, the word "drought" means a dry spell. It refers to a period of time when there is little or no rain, which can lead to dry conditions and a lack of water. The other choices, A) heavy rain, C) cold weather, and D) forest fire, are incorrect because they do not capture the meaning of the word "drought" as it is used in this passage. The passage tells us that a drought hit the land, causing the crops to suffer and the people to worry. This indicates that there was a lack of rain and dry conditions, rather than heavy rain, cold weather, or a forest fire. Therefore, the correct answer is B) dry spell, as it best describes the meaning of "drought" in this context.

www.math-knots.com | www.a4ace.com

6. Answer: **D. He turned into a smaller creature and flew into the heavens**

Explanation: After helping the people, Long did not leave on a boat, as mentioned in choice A), and there is no mention of him going back to his cave, as stated in choice C). Furthermore, he did not disappear into thin air, as mentioned in choice B). Instead, the passage tells us that Long turned into a smaller creature and flew into the heavens. This means that choice D) "He turned into a smaller creature and flew into the heavens" is the correct answer. The story indicates that Long transformed into a dragonfly, a smaller creature, and ascended into the sky, symbolizing his departure. Therefore, the correct answer is D) based on the information provided in the passage.

7. Answer: **D. He was a powerful dragon who controlled the water and brought good luck and fortune.**

Explanation: The passage states that Long, the dragon, was known as the most powerful and divine creature in China. It also mentions that Long could control water, make it rain, and bring good luck to the farmers' crops. Therefore, choice A accurately describes Long's role in China as a powerful dragon who had the ability to control water and bring luck and fortune. Choice B is incorrect because Long was not a farmer but a dragon. Choice C is partially correct as Long was a symbol of the emperor but it does not capture his ability to control water and bring luck. Choice D is incorrect because Long turned into a dragonfly after helping the people, but it does not describe his role accurately.

8. Answer: **C. Dragons were symbols of luck and good fortune.**

Explanation: The passage mentions that dragons were the symbol of the emperor and brought luck and good fortune. This indicates that in Chinese culture, dragons held symbolic significance associated with positive aspects such as luck and good fortune. Option A, that dragons were the rulers of China, is not supported by the information provided in the passage. Option B, that dragons were the protectors of the emperor, is not explicitly mentioned in the passage. Option D, that dragons brought destruction, is contrary to the positive role attributed to dragons in Chinese culture as stated in the passage.

9. Answer: **B. Repeat.**

Explanation: The prefix "re-" in the word "remembered" indicates a repetition or an action being done again. In this context, "remembered" means that Long will always be thought of or recalled as the mighty dragon who brought good luck and fortune to the people of China. It implies that his memory or reputation will be repeated or kept alive in people's minds. Choice A, "Forget," is incorrect because it has the opposite meaning of what the prefix suggests. Choice C, "Repair," and choice D, "Remove," are not related to the prefix "re-" and do not accurately reflect its meaning in this context.

www.math-knots.com | www.a4ace.com

The Boy Who Cried Wolf

10. Answer: B. To watch over his family's sheep

Explanation: Jack's job was to watch over his family's sheep, as mentioned in the passage. He had the responsibility of ensuring the safety of the sheep from wolves and other predators. This aligns with choice B) "To watch over his family's sheep." The other choices, A) "To watch over his family's pigs" and C) "To watch over his family's horses," are incorrect because the passage specifically states that Jack's job was to watch over the sheep, not pigs or horses. Therefore, the correct answer is B) "To watch over his family's sheep" based on the information provided in the passage.

11. Answer: A. dangerous and hazardous

Explanation: In the context of the story, the word "treacherous" means dangerous and hazardous. It describes the nature of the wolves and other predators that Jack had to protect the sheep from. The word "treacherous" suggests that these animals posed a threat to the safety of the sheep and could potentially cause harm. The other choices, B) friendly and welcoming and C) peaceful and serene, are incorrect because they do not capture the meaning of the word "treacherous" as it is used in this context. The passage emphasizes the need for Jack to protect the sheep from dangerous predators, indicating that the correct answer is A) dangerous and hazardous.

12. Answer: B. The villagers did not believe Jack and the wolf ate several of his sheep

Explanation: When a real wolf attacked Jack's sheep, the villagers did not believe Jack's cries for help, resulting in the wolf eating several of his sheep. This aligns with choice B) "The villagers did not believe Jack and the wolf ate several of his sheep." The passage explains that because Jack had lied to the villagers multiple times before, they had stopped believing him even when a real danger occurred. As a consequence, the wolf was able to harm the sheep because the villagers did not come to Jack's aid. Choice A) "The villagers believed Jack and helped him protect his sheep" is incorrect because it contradicts the information given in the passage. Likewise, choice C) "Jack was able to protect all of his sheep from the wolf" is also incorrect because the passage clearly states that the wolf ate several of Jack's sheep due to the villagers' disbelief. Therefore, the correct answer is B) based on the events described in the story.

13. Answer: A. Thwart

Explanation: The word in the story that means "to prevent or stop from happening" is A) Thwart. In the context of the story, thwart means to hinder or obstruct, preventing something from taking place. This aligns with the meaning of "to prevent or stop from happening." The other choices, B) Wane and C) Fortify, do not carry the same meaning. Wane means to decrease or diminish, while fortify means to strengthen or reinforce. These words do not convey the idea of preventing or stopping something from happening. Therefore, the correct answer is A) Thwart based on its definition and relevance to the given context.

14. Answer: A. He was bored

Explanation: Jack decided to play a trick on the villagers because he was bored, as mentioned in the passage. Choice A) "He was bored" aligns with the reason stated in the story. Jack's boredom led him to seek amusement by playing a prank on the villagers. The other choices, B) "He wanted to make them angry" and C) "He was hungry," are incorrect because they do not reflect the motivation given in the passage. There is no indication that Jack's intention was to make the villagers angry, nor is there any mention of hunger being a factor in his decision. Therefore, the correct answer is A) "He was bored" based on the information provided in the passage.

 www.math-knots.com | www.a4ace.com

15. Answer: **C. "Wolf, wolf! A wolf is attacking my sheep!"**

Explanation: When Jack ran into the village, he shouted, "Wolf, wolf! A wolf is attacking my sheep!" This aligns with choice C) "Wolf, wolf! A wolf is attacking my sheep!" The passage explicitly states that Jack used the word "wolf" to describe the threat to his sheep. The other choices, A) "Bear, bear! A bear is attacking my sheep!" and B) "Tiger, tiger! A tiger is attacking my sheep!" are incorrect because they do not reflect what Jack actually shouted in the story. There is no mention of bears or tigers, only wolves, as being the predators that Jack pretended to warn the villagers about. Therefore, the correct answer is C) "Wolf, wolf! A wolf is attacking my sheep!" based on the information provided in the passage.

16. Answer: **B. Annoyed**

Explanation: The villagers felt annoyed after Jack played his trick on them several times, as mentioned in the passage. Choice B) "Annoyed" aligns with the emotions expressed by the villagers in response to Jack's repeated pranks. The passage states that although the villagers came to help Jack every time he cried out for a wolf, they eventually grew tired of his deceit. The other choices, A) "Happy" and C) "Excited," are incorrect because they do not reflect the negative sentiment of annoyance that the villagers experienced. The passage emphasizes the villagers' frustration with Jack's repeated tricks, indicating that the correct answer is B) "Annoyed" based on the information provided in the passage.

17. Answer: **C. That being truthful is important for others to trust you.**

Explanation: Jack learned the lesson that being truthful is important for others to trust you, as stated in the passage. Choice C) "That being truthful is important for others to trust you" aligns with the moral of the story. Jack's repeated lies and tricks caused the villagers to lose trust in him, leading to dire consequences when a real wolf attacked his sheep. Jack realized the negative impact of his dishonesty and made a promise to be truthful from then on. The other choices, A) "To always play tricks on people" and B) "That it is okay to lie to get attention," are incorrect because they go against the moral lesson of the story. The story teaches the importance of honesty and the consequences of deceit, not the encouragement of playing tricks or lying for attention. Therefore, the correct answer is C) "That being truthful is important for others to trust you" based on the message conveyed in the passage.

Jimia's Brave Adventure

18. Answer: **C. Going to an adventure park**

Explanation: Jimia's class planned to go to an adventure park for their field trip, as stated in the passage. Choice C) "Going to an adventure park" aligns with the specific activity mentioned in the story. The passage mentions that the adventure park had a high rope course that challenged people to overcome their fears, which indicates that it was an outdoor recreational facility suitable for adventurous activities. The other choices, A) "Going to the zoo," B) "Visiting a museum," and D) "Watching a movie," are incorrect because they are not mentioned or implied in the passage. Therefore, the correct answer is C) "Going to an adventure park" based on the information provided in the paragraph.

19. Answer: **C. Heights**

Explanation: According to paragraph 3, Jimia was scared of heights, as mentioned in the passage. Choice C) "Heights" aligns with the specific fear stated in the story. It is mentioned that Jimia felt scared and her heart would race and legs would tremble whenever she had to climb even a small ladder or go near a balcony. This fear of heights is the focus of her secret fear that she wished to overcome. The other choices, A) "Water," B) "Animals," and D) "Darkness," are incorrect because they are not mentioned or implied as Jimia's fear in the given paragraph. Therefore, the correct answer is C) "Heights" based on the information provided.

20. Answer: **B. Paragraph 3**

Explanation: Jimia climbed up the ladder to start the rope course in paragraph 3, as mentioned in the passage. Choice B) "Paragraph 3" aligns with the specific paragraph where Jimia's ascent to the rope course is described. In that paragraph, it is stated that Jimia took a deep breath, climbed up the ladder, and started navigating the course. The other choices, A) "Paragraph 2," C) "Paragraph 4," and D) "Paragraph 5," are incorrect because they do not correspond to the specific paragraph where Jimia's climb is described. Therefore, the correct answer is B) "Paragraph 3" based on the information provided.

21. Answer: **A. The support of her classmates and teacher**

Explanation: According to paragraph 4, what helped Jimia gather the courage to start the rope course was the support of her classmates and the encouraging words from her teacher, as mentioned in the passage. Choice A) "The support of her classmates and teacher" aligns with the specific factor mentioned in the story that contributed to Jimia's courage. It is stated that with the support of her classmates and the encouraging words from her teacher, Jimia climbed up the ladder and started navigating the course. The other choices, B) "Seeing her friends complete the course," C) "A magic potion she drank," and D) "Her favorite music playing in the background," are incorrect because they are not mentioned or implied as factors that helped Jimia gather the courage to start the rope course. Therefore, the correct answer is A) "The support of her classmates and teacher" based on the information provided in the paragraph.

22. Answer: **C. Her confidence grew**

Explanation: According to paragraph 5, as Jimia faced each obstacle in the rope course, her confidence grew, as mentioned in the passage. Choice C) "Her confidence grew" aligns with the specific emotion described in the story. It is stated that with every step, her confidence grew as she faced her fear head-on, one obstacle at a time. The other choices, A) "She became more scared," B) "She gave up and went back down," and D) "She asked for help from her teacher," are incorrect because they do not reflect the emotional progression mentioned in the paragraph. Instead, the paragraph emphasizes Jimia's increasing confidence as she tackled each obstacle. Therefore, the correct answer is C) "Her confidence grew" based on the information provided.

23. Answer: **C. Paragraph 4**

Explanation: According to paragraph 4, Jimia's friends cheered her on as she navigated the rope course. It is stated that Jimia's friends cheered her on, indicating their support and encouragement during her journey. The other choices, A) Paragraph 2, B) Paragraph 3, and D) Paragraph 5, are incorrect because they do not describe the specific moment when Jimia's friends cheered her on. Therefore, the correct answer is C) Paragraph 4 based on the information provided.

www.math-knots.com | www.a4ace.com

24. Answer: **B. Proud and accomplished**

Explanation: According to paragraph 5, after conquering her fear, Jimia felt proud and accomplished, as mentioned in the passage. It is stated that as Jimia climbed back down, she felt proud and accomplished. This indicates that she had a positive and fulfilling experience. The other choices, A) "Angry," C) "Disappointed," and D) "Sad and scared," are incorrect because they do not align with the emotions described in the paragraph. The passage emphasizes Jimia's sense of pride and accomplishment, highlighting her positive feelings after facing her fear. Therefore, the correct answer is B) "Proud and accomplished" based on the information provided.

25. Answer: **C. It meant facing fears with courage**

Explanation: According to paragraph 5, Jimia realized that being brave meant facing fears with courage. It is stated that Jimia learned that being brave wasn't about never being scared but facing fears with courage. This indicates that Jimia understood that bravery involves confronting and overcoming fears rather than avoiding or eliminating them. The other choices, A) "It meant never feeling scared," B) "It meant avoiding challenges," and D) "It meant always winning," are incorrect because they do not reflect the lesson that Jimia learned as described in the paragraph. Therefore, the correct answer is C) "It meant facing fears with courage" based on the information provided.

26. Answer: **C. Paragraph 4**

Explanation: Jimia reached the final platform of the rope course in paragraph 4. It is mentioned that with every step, her confidence grew, and she faced her fear head-on, overcoming one obstacle at a time. Her friends cheered her on, and eventually, she reached the final platform. The paragraph describes how Jimia looked down and smiled from the top, indicating that she had successfully completed the course. Therefore, the correct answer is C) Paragraph 4. The other choices are incorrect because paragraph 2 talks about the planning of the field trip, paragraph 3 describes Jimia deciding to give the rope course a try, and paragraph 5 mentions Jimia climbing back down and feeling proud and accomplished, but it does not mention reaching the final platform.

How The Camel Got His Hump

27. Answer: **B. Making loud howling sounds**

Explanation: According to the story, the Camel was known for making loud howling sounds among the animals. In paragraph 1, it is mentioned that the Camel didn't want to work and was lazy. Instead of doing useful tasks like the other animals, he would eat sticks, thorns, tamarisks, and prickles, and make howling sounds. Whenever anyone tried to talk to him, all he would say was "Humph!" This shows that the Camel's distinct characteristic was making loud howling sounds. Therefore, the correct answer is B) Making loud howling sounds. The other choices are incorrect because the story portrays the Camel as lazy and unproductive, not as a hard worker or someone who helps others. Additionally, there is no mention of the Camel eating grass specifically.

www.math-knots.com | www.a4ace.com

28. Answer: **C. To invite him to trot like the others**

Explanation: The Horse approached the Camel to invite him to trot like the rest of the animals. In paragraph 2, it is mentioned that the Horse had a saddle on his back and a bit in his mouth, indicating that he was prepared for a ride. The Horse wanted the Camel to join in and be productive like the others. However, the Camel responded with his usual lazy "Humph!" This shows that the Horse approached the Camel with the intention of inviting him to trot and contribute like everyone else. Therefore, the correct answer is C) To invite him to trot like the others. The other choices are incorrect because there is no mention of a race, the Horse asking for a ride, or complaining about the weather in the context of the story.

29. Answer: **A. The Dog**

Explanation: In the story, it is mentioned in paragraph 3 that the Dog came to the Camel carrying a stick and insisted that he should come and fetch and carry like the others. The Dog tried to persuade the Camel to work by urging him to participate in useful tasks. Therefore, the correct answer is A) The Dog. The other choices are incorrect because there is no mention of the Owl, the Djinn, or the Man trying to persuade the Camel to work in the context of the story.

30. Answer: **B. "Humph!"**

Explanation: In the story, it is mentioned in paragraph 4 that when the Ox approached the Camel with a yoke on his neck, inviting him to come and plow like the rest, the Camel responded with his usual lazy and nonchalant "Humph!" Therefore, the correct answer is B) "Humph!" The other choices are incorrect as they do not match the response given by the Camel in the story.

31. Answer: **C. Because the world was new and needed everyone's contribution.**

Explanation: In paragraph 5 of the story, the Man called the Horse, the Dog, and the Ox together and expressed his regret that the world was new and needed everyone's contribution. He acknowledged that the Camel was an idle creature and could not be forced to work. Therefore, he instructed the Horse, the Dog, and the Ox to work twice as hard to make up for the Camel's laziness. This shows that the reason for the instruction was that the world needed everyone to contribute their efforts. The other choices are incorrect because they do not align with the information provided in the story. The decision was not made because the camel was their friend, to impress the djinn, or because they were the strongest animals.

32. Answer: **A. The Djinn.**

Explanation: In paragraph 6 of the story, a Djinn, who was in charge of all the deserts, appeared in a cloud of dust. The Horse approached the Djinn and voiced his concern about the Camel's idleness. Therefore, the Djinn is the one who appeared to address the Camel's laziness. The other choices are incorrect because the Man, the Horse, and the Dog did not appear in a cloud of dust to address the issue.

33. Answer: **B. He had to carry a hump on his back.**

Explanation: In paragraph 7 of the story, the Djinn, who was in charge of all the deserts, identified the Camel as the culprit. The Horse mentioned the Camel's unhelpful response, and the Dog and the Ox added that he wouldn't fetch, carry, or plow either. As a punishment for his idle behavior, the Djinn decided to make the Camel carry a hump on his back. This consequence is mentioned in the story. The other choices are incorrect because the Camel was not banished from the desert, he did not become the leader of the other animals, and he did not receive a reward for his laziness.

                   www.math-knots.com | www.a4ace.com

34. Answer: A. "All he would say was, 'Humph!' and nothing more."

This sentence describes the Camel's response whenever someone tried to talk to him. He would simply say "Humph!" and not engage further. This indicates his lack of interest or willingness to work or participate in any activities. The other options (B, C, and D) mention other characters approaching the Camel with objects related to work, but they do not explicitly suggest the Camel's unwillingness to work like the sentence in option A.

35. Answer: A. Why did the Horse approach the Camel?

In paragraph 2, it is mentioned that the Horse approached the Camel with a saddle on his back and a bit in his mouth, urging him to come out and trot like the rest of them. However, the Camel responded with his usual "Humph!" This indicates that the Horse approached the Camel to encourage him to join and participate in the activities like trotting. Therefore, paragraph 2 answers the question of why the Horse approached the Camel. The other options (B, C, and D) are not addressed in paragraph 2.

The Mysterious Move and the Curious Imp

36. Answer: C. Unhappy

According to the passage, Celeste feels unhappy about the house she is supposed to move into. The text mentions that when Celeste sees the house, she realizes it is a run-down ramshackle place that needs a wrecking ball instead of a mop. This shows that she is not happy with the condition of the house. The other choices, A. Excited and B. Happy, are incorrect because the passage clearly states that Celeste is not happy about the house. Therefore, the correct answer is C. Unhappy.

37. Answer: C. A wrecking ball

The house in the story could use a wrecking ball instead of just a mop. The passage mentions that the house is described as a "run-down ramshackle place," implying that it is in a very poor condition. A wrecking ball is a heavy tool used to demolish buildings that are beyond repair. While options A (New windows), B (A fresh coat of paint), and D (A new kitchen) suggest possible improvements; they do not capture the extent of the house's dilapidation. Therefore, they are not the most suitable choices for addressing the house's condition. The correct answer is C (A wrecking ball) as it aligns with the description of the house needing more than just a mop for its improvement.

38. Answer: D. None of the above

The passage does not explicitly mention the reason why Celeste's mother wants to move to Cripley Hollow. Therefore, the correct answer is D (None of the above) as there is no information provided to support options A, B, or C.

39. Answer: B. Grumblemunch

Based on the information provided in the passage, the correct answer is B (Grumblemunch). The passage mentions that Grumblemunch, the imp who has lived in the cellar of the old house for decades, is unhappy about the move. There is no mention of Celeste's father or sister being unhappy about the move, so option A (Celeste's father) and option C (Celeste's sister) are incorrect.

78

40. Answer: **A. The basement**

Grumblemunch, the imp, lives in the cellar of the old house. The cellar is a part of the house that is usually underground or below the main level. This is where Grumblemunch has made his home and collected all the junk he loves. The other choices are incorrect because the passage specifically mentions that Grumblemunch lives in the cellar, not in the attic, backyard, or shed. Therefore, the correct answer is A) The basement.

41. Answer: **C. Junk**

Grumblemunch, the imp, loves to collect junk. The passage states that he enjoys running through the tall grass and has collected a lot of junk in the cellar of the old house where he lives. This indicates that Grumblemunch has a fondness for gathering and keeping various objects that others might consider useless or unwanted. Therefore, the correct answer is C) Junk.

42. Answer: **C) running around**

Grumblemunch, the imp likes to run around in the tall grass. The passage mentions that he enjoys "running through the tall grass," indicating that he finds pleasure in moving around and being active in that environment. Therefore, the correct answer is C) running around. This choice reflects Grumblemunch's energetic behavior and suggests that he enjoys exploring and playing in the tall grass. The other choices, A) chase butterflies and B) eat insects, are not specifically mentioned in the passage, so they cannot be determined as activities Grumblemunch engages in.

43. Answer: **B) New people are moving into the house.**

Everything is changing for Grumblemunch because new people are moving into the house. In the passage, it is mentioned that Celeste and her mother are headed toward their new home in Cripley Hollow. This implies that the old house, where Grumblemunch has lived for decades, will no longer be his home. The arrival of new people signifies a significant change in his living situation. Therefore, the correct answer is B) New people are moving into the house. The other choices, A) His favorite tree was cut down and C) His collection got ruined, are not mentioned in the given passage and cannot be determined as reasons for the changes affecting Grumblemunch.

Weaving of Kente Cloth Taught by a Spider

44. Answer: **A) Silk and cotton**

Kente cloth is made of silk and cotton. According to the passage, Kente cloth is a type of fabric made of interwoven cloth strips and is native to the Akan ethnic group. The correct answer is A) Silk and cotton. The other choices, B) Wool and linen, C) Polyester and nylon, and D) Velvet and silk, are not mentioned in the passage and cannot be determined as materials used to make Kente cloth. The passage specifically states that Kente cloth is made of silk and cotton, which are the materials traditionally used in its production.

45. Answer: **A) Black and white fibers**

According to the passage, the brothers used black and white fibers obtained from the raffia tree to make their first cloth. This information is explicitly mentioned in paragraph 3. Therefore, the correct answer is A) Black and white fibers. The other choices, B) Silk and cotton threads, C) Raffia tree leaves, and D) Spider silk, are all incorrect because they are not mentioned in the passage as the materials used by the brothers to create the cloth.

     www.math-knots.com | www.a4ace.com

46. Answer: **B. A spider**

According to the passage, Kurugu and Ameyaw found a spider while they were hunting. This information is mentioned in paragraph 2, where it states that during their journey, they came across a remarkable sight—a spider meticulously weaving an extraordinary web. Therefore, the correct answer is B) A spider. The other choices, A) A treasure chest, C) A rare flower, and D) A secret passage, are all incorrect because they are not mentioned in the passage as what the brothers found during their hunting expedition.

47. Answer: **D) The history and significance of Kente cloth**

The main idea of the passage is D) The history and significance of Kente cloth. The passage provides information about the origins of Kente cloth, its cultural and historical importance, its association with the Akan people's royalty and heritage, and its evolution over time. It discusses how Kente cloth is made, its symbolism, and its continued reverence in Ghana and around the world. While the other options may be mentioned or touched upon in the passage, they are not the central focus or main idea of the text.

48. Answer: **B) To sew together**

The word "interwoven" means B) To sew together in the context of the passage. It refers to the process of combining and intertwining cloth strips to create Kente cloth. It implies that the cloth strips are skillfully woven together, forming intricate patterns and designs. The word "interwoven" suggests a sense of unity and integration, highlighting the weaving technique used to create the fabric. The other options, such as tearing apart, mixing colors, or cutting into strips, do not accurately capture the meaning of "interwoven" in this context.

49. Answer: **C) Picture of Kings**

The correct answer is C) Picture of Kings. In the passage, it is mentioned that in the past, Kente cloth was exclusively reserved for special occasions and festivities, and only kings had the privilege of wearing it. Therefore, the picture of kings represents the individuals who used to wear Kente cloth during such occasions. The other options, including men and women, children and elders, and holy animals, do not accurately represent the specific group mentioned in the passage.

50. Answer: **D. The detailed workings or processes**

The correct answer is D) The detailed workings or processes. In the context of the passage, the word "mechanics" refers to the intricate details and processes involved in the weaving technique observed by Kurugu and Ameyaw. They carefully observed the mechanics of the spider's weaving process, which means they observed the detailed workings and processes of how the spider weaved its web. The other options, such as people who repair machines, the study of motion and forces, and tools and equipment used for weaving, do not accurately capture the meaning of "mechanics" as used in this context.

YOUNG GEORGE AND THE COLT –

BY HORACE SCUDDER

1. **B) Sorrel.**

Sorrel is a reddish-brown color. The story tells us that the horse was described as a spirited sorrel, meaning it had a fiery and energetic nature. The other choices are incorrect because A) Bay refers to a brown horse with a black mane and tail, C) Chestnut refers to a reddish-brown color without a black mane and tail, and D) Black refers to a horse that is entirely black in color. In the story, it is clearly mentioned that George Washington wanted to ride a horse that was described as sorrel, so the answer is B) Sorrel.

2. **C) To maintain their bloodline.**

George Washington's mother took pains to keep the stock of horses pure because she wanted to maintain the bloodline. This means she wanted to ensure that the horses came from a specific lineage or breed without mixing it with other breeds. By keeping the bloodline pure, she could preserve the desired characteristics, qualities, and traits of the horses she owned. This was important to her as a horse breeder, as maintaining a pure bloodline often ensures the continuation of certain desirable traits from generation to generation. The other choices are incorrect because there is no mention in the story that George Washington's mother kept the horses pure for the purpose of winning horse racing competitions, selling them at a higher price, or preventing them from being classified as vicious.

3. **B) His friends distracted the colt while he mounted it.**

In the story, it is mentioned that George Washington's friends helped him catch the spirited colt. They surrounded the colt and managed to put a bit into its mouth. With his friends' assistance, George Washington was able to mount the colt while it was distracted by the other boys. This allowed him to get on the colt's back and begin his attempt to ride and tame it. The other choices are incorrect because there is no mention of George Washington using a lasso to catch the colt, bribing the colt with treats, or training the colt using a gentle approach.

4. **D) It died from a burst blood vessel.**

During George Washington's attempt to tame the spirited colt, there was a struggle between them. The colt resisted and exhibited aggressive behavior, including backing about the field, rearing, and plunging. The climax of the struggle occurred when the colt leaped into the air with a tremendous bound, causing a burst blood vessel. As a result, the colt tragically died. This turn of events led to the horse's demise rather than it throwing George Washington off and escaping, surrendering, and becoming docile, or falling ill and needing medical attention.

5. **D) They were unsure of the fate of the other colts.**

The boys hesitated to speak when George Washington's mother asked about her colts because they were unsure of the fate of the other colts. They had witnessed the spirited colt's struggle with George Washington and saw it tragically die. Since they were not certain about the well-being of the other colts, they hesitated togive a definite answer to George Washington's mother. This uncertainty made them hesitant to speak up. The other choices may also be plausible, but based on the context of the story, the most direct reason for their hesitation is the uncertainty about the other colts.

6. C) His truthfulness and honesty.

Despite the loss of her favorite colt, George Washington's mother admired his truthfulness and honesty. When George Washington informed his mother that he was responsible for the colt's death and shared the whole story, his mother, after initially feeling anger, controlled herself and acknowledged that while she regretted the loss of her favorite horse, she rejoiced in her son who always spoke the truth. This indicates that his mother valued and appreciated George Washington's honesty and truthfulness, even in a difficult situation. The other choices, such as his riding skills, ability to control the colt, and determination to tame the colt, are not explicitly mentioned as the qualities his mother specifically admired in this particular context of the story.

7. A) A lively, untamed horse with a fiery expression and lifted hooves.

Explanation: The sentence that best represents the spirited sorrel colt that George Washington wanted to ride is A - A lively, untamed horse with a fiery expression and lifted hooves. In the story, it mentions that the colt was described as spirited and extremely spirited, which means it was full of energy and had a lot of spirit. The sentence describes a horse that matches this description with its lively appearance, fiery expression, and lifted hooves. The other choices are incorrect because B) A calm, gentle horse peacefully grazing in a pasture describes a horse that is calm and gentle, which doesn't match the description of the spirited colt. C) A tired, exhausted horse resting in a stable describes a horse that is tired and resting, which doesn't match the energetic nature of the colt. D) A horse being trained and ridden by a professional equestrian describes a horse that is being trained and ridden by someone, which doesn't represent the untamed nature of the colt. Therefore, the correct answer is A) as it best represents the spirited sorrel colt described in the story.

8. D) The colt lying lifeless on the ground after a burst blood vessel.

Explanation: The sentence that depicts the final moment of the colt's struggle with George Washington is D) The colt lying lifeless on the ground after a burst blood vessel. In the story, it states that during their struggle, the colt made a tremendous leap into the air, which caused a burst blood vessel. As a result, the colt tragically died. The sentence accurately represents this final moment with the colt lying lifeless on the ground. The other choices are incorrect because A) George Washington firmly seated on the colt while it rears up in defiance does not reflect the colt's demise. B) The colt successfully throwing off George Washington and galloping away does not show the colt's fate accurately. C) George Washington and the colt peacefully standing side by side after taming does not depict the outcome of the struggle, where the colt dies. Therefore, the correct answer is D) as it depicts the final moment of the colt's struggle as described in the story.

THE STORY OF THE INKY BOYS - HEINRICH HOFFMANN

9. B) His green umbrella.

In the poem, it mentions that the Black-a-moor took his green umbrella with him on his outing. The line "He took with him his green umbrella" explicitly states that the umbrella he brought was green. Therefore, the correct answer is B) His green umbrella. The other choices are incorrect because the poem does not mention the Black-a-moor taking a black umbrella, a wooden hoop, or a jacket with him on his outing.

10. **A) Arthur.**

In the poem, it is mentioned that Edward, a little noisy wag, ran out, laughed, and waved his flag. The poem then continues by stating, "And William came in jacket trim, And brought his wooden hoop with him; And Arthur, too, snatched up his toys And joined the other naughty boys." From this, we can infer that Arthur joined Edward in waving a flag. Therefore, the correct answer is A) Arthur. The other choices, B) William, C) The Black-a-moor, and D) No one, are incorrect based on the information provided in the poem.

11. **A) His wooden hoop.**

In the poem, it states, "And William came in jacket trim, And brought his wooden hoop with him." This clearly mentions that William brought his wooden hoop with him. Therefore, the correct answer is A) His wooden hoop. The other choices, B) His green umbrella, C) His jacket, and D) His toys, are incorrect as they do not match what William specifically brought according to the poem.

12. **A) They laughed and hooted.**

In the poem, it mentions that the other boys, Edward, William, and Arthur, reacted to the Black-a-moor by laughing and hooting. The line states, "one and all set up a roar, and laughed and hooted more and more." This indicates that the boys responded to the Black-a-moor by laughing and hooting. Therefore, the correct answer is A) They laughed and hooted. The other choices, B) They sang a song, C) They waved their flags, and D) They joined him for a walk, are incorrect as they do not match the reaction described in the poem.

13. **C) His black color.**

In the poem, it mentions that the boys teased the Black-a-moor by singing, "Oh, Blacky, you're as black as ink!" This indicates that the teasing was directed towards the Black-a-moor's black color. Therefore, the correct answer is C) His black color. The other choices, A) His toys, B) His flag, and D) His umbrella, are incorrect as they do not match the specific teasing mentioned in the poem.

14. **D) His feelings were not mentioned.**

Explanation: The poem does not mention how the Black-a-moor felt about the teasing. It does not provide any information about his response or feelings towards the teasing. Therefore, the correct answer is D) His feelings were not mentioned. The other choices are incorrect because A) He ignored it assumes that the Black-a-moor chose to ignore the teasing, B) He joined in the laughter assumes that he participated in the teasing by laughing, and C) He waved his flag in response assumes that he responded to the teasing by waving his flag. These choices are not supported by the information given in the poem, where it does not specify the Black-a-moor's reaction or feelings towards the teasing.

15. **C) Hot.**

Explanation: The poem mentions that the Black-a-moor went out on a "nice fine summer's day." This indicates that the weather on that day was hot. Therefore, the correct answer is C) Hot. The other choices, A) Rainy, B) Snowy, and D) Windy, are incorrect because the poem does not mention any rainy, snowy, or windy conditions. The description of a "nice fine summer's day" implies a pleasant and warm weather, suggesting that it was a hot day. Therefore, the correct answer is C) Hot based on the information provided in the poem.

16. **A) Black as ink.**

Explanation: In the poem, the Black-a-moor is described as being "Black as ink." This indicates that the color of the Black-a-moor is black. Therefore, the correct answer is A) Black as ink. The other choices, B) Green, C) Woolly-headed, and D) Not mentioned, are incorrect. The poem specifically mentions the Black a-moor's black color by comparing it to the color of ink. The choice B) Green is incorrect because the poem does not mention the Black-a-moor being green. The choice C) Woolly-headed is incorrect because it refers to the Black-a-moor's hair texture and not its color. The choice D) Not mentioned is incorrect because the poem provides a direct description of the Black-a-moor's color as black.

THE BLUE BIRD – BY MAURICE-MAETERLINCK
AND GEORGETTE-LEBLANC

17. **B) Daddy Tyl could not go to work in the forest.**

In the story, it is mentioned that Mummy Tyl felt a little sad on Christmas Eve because Daddy Tyl was unable to go to work in the forest due to the stormy weather. This implies that the family was facing financial difficulties since Daddy Tyl couldn't work, and as a result, Mummy Tyl had no money to buy presents for the children. Therefore, the correct answer is B) Daddy Tyl could not go to work in the forest. The other choices, A) The children were misbehaving, C) The weather was stormy, and D) The children were not asleep, are incorrect as they are not mentioned in the passage as reasons for Mummy Tyl feeling sad on Christmas Eve.

18. **D) Laughter of the children.**

In the passage, it is mentioned that as the children fell asleep, the sound of the purring cat, the snoring dog, and the ticking of the great grandfather's clock could be heard. However, there is no mention of the laughter of the children. Therefore, the correct answer is D) Laughter of the children. The other choices, A) Purring of the cat, B) Snoring of the dog, and C) Ticking of the great grandfather's clock, are incorrect as they are specifically mentioned in the passage as sounds that were heard in the room.

19. **B) 2.**

In the sentence, "the two Children awoke, yawned, rubbed their eyes, stretched out their arms in bed," the meaning of "arm" that is used refers to each of the upper two limbs of the children. It indicates that the children extended their arms while they were in bed. Therefore, the correct answer is B) 2. The other choices, A) 1 - a sleeve of a garment, C) 3 - used to refer to something powerful or protective, and D) 4 - a side part of a chair, do not match the context of the sentence and are unrelated to the action of the children stretching out their limbs.

20. **A) A bright light creeping through the shutters.**

The passage says that the children woke up because a very bright light came through the window. The other choices are incorrect because the passage does not mention any loud noise from outside, Mummy Tyl calling them, or Father Christmas entering the room. It is important to read the passage carefully to find the answer.

www.math-knots.com | www.a4ace.com

21. **A) He overheard his parents talking.**

Explanation: Tyltyl knew that Father Christmas wouldn't bring them anything that year because he overheard his parents talking. In the story, it is mentioned that Tyltyl's mother, Mummy Tyl, couldn't go to town to tell Father Christmas about their wishes for presents. Tyltyl heard his mother say this, which made him realize that Father Christmas wouldn't be able to bring them gifts. This is why option A is the correct answer. Option B, "The shutters were closed," is incorrect because the closed shutters have nothing to do with Tyltyl's knowledge about Father Christmas. They only serve as a visual cue for the bright lights coming from the rich children's house. Option C, "His sister told him," is incorrect because there is no mention in the passage of Mytyl, Tyltyl's sister, telling him about Father Christmas not coming that year. Option D, "He saw the lights of the party at the rich children's house," is a tempting dis-tractor but ultimately incorrect. Although Tyltyl does see the lights of the party at the rich children's house, this observation does not provide any information about Father Christmas not bringing them gifts. The knowledge about Father Christmas not coming is based on Tyltyl overhearing his parents' conversation, as explained in option A.

22. **D) To see the Christmas tree at the party.**

Explanation: Tyltyl wanted to get up and open the shutters to see the Christmas tree at the party. In the passage, Tyltyl notices the bright lights coming from the rich children's house, where a Christmas tree is being celebrated. He refers to it as a party and suggests opening the shutters to get a better view of the Christmas tree. Therefore, option D is the correct answer.

Option A, "To see if it was Christmas Day," is incorrect because Tyltyl and his sister already knew it was Christmas Eve, as mentioned in the passage. They were aware that Christmas Day would be the following day. Option B, "To turn off the lamp," is incorrect because there is no indication in the passage that Tyltyl wanted to turn off the lamp. The lamp was mentioned to have lit up on its own when the bright light crept through the shutters. Option C, "To look for Father Christmas," is incorrect because there is no mention of Tyltyl wanting to look for Father Christmas at that moment. His desire to open the shutters was primarily to see the Christmas tree at the party, as stated in option D.

23. **B) She thought they shouldn't get out of bed.**

Explanation: Mytyl hesitated to get up because she thought they shouldn't get out of bed. In the passage, it is mentioned that Mytyl always remembered that they mustn't get up. She was aware of the rule or expectation that they should stay in bed during that time. Therefore, option B is the correct answer.

Option A, "She was afraid of the dark," is incorrect because there is no mention of Mytyl being afraid of the dark in the given passage. Fear of the dark is not provided as a reason for her hesitation. Option C, "She was waiting for Father Christmas," is incorrect because there is no mention of Mytyl waiting for Father Christmas in the passage. The focus of the passage is on Tyltyl's awareness that Father Christmas wouldn't bring them gifts that year. Option D, "She wanted to play with the rich children," is incorrect because there is no indication in the passage that Mytyl wanted to play with the rich children. The passage focuses on their observation of the lights and the Christmas tree at the party, but there is no mention of Mytyl's desire to play with the rich children.

         www.math-knots.com | www.a4ace.com

24. A) The Christmas tree at the party.

Explanation: Tyltyl thought that the bright lights were from the Christmas tree at the party. In the passage, Tyltyl notices the bright lights coming from the rich children's house and refers to it as a party. He assumes that the lights are from the Christmas tree at that party. Therefore, option A is the correct answer.

Option B, "The moon shining through the shutters," is incorrect because there is no mention of the moon in the passage. The source of the bright lights is specifically attributed to the party and the Christmas tree, not the moon. Option C, "Fireworks outside," is incorrect because there is no mention of fireworks in the passage. The bright lights are not associated with fireworks but with the Christmas tree at the party. Option D, "Mummy Tyl's candles," is incorrect because there is no mention of Mummy Tyl's candles in the passage. The bright lights are separate from any candles and are specifically attributed to the party and the Christmas tree.

25. C) The rich children playing with their gifts.

Explanation: Tyltyl and Mytyl expected to see the rich children playing with their gifts when they opened the shutters. In the passage, Tyltyl mentions the bright lights coming from the rich children's house, which he identifies as a party with a Christmas tree. The anticipation of opening the shutters is driven by their curiosity to observe the scene at the party, where the rich children would be playing with their gifts. Therefore, option C is the correct answer.

Option A, "Father Christmas delivering presents," is incorrect because there is no mention of Tyltyl and Mytyl expecting to see Father Christmas delivering presents. Their understanding, as mentioned in the passage, is that Father Christmas wouldn't bring them anything that year. Option B, "A snowy landscape," is incorrect because there is no indication of Tyltyl and Mytyl expecting to see a snowy landscape when they open the shutters. The focus of their expectation is specifically on the rich children and the gifts they are playing with. Option D, "Mummy Tyl lighting candles," is incorrect because there is no mention of Tyltyl and Mytyl expecting to see Mummy Tyl lighting candles when they open the shutters. The primary interest lies in observing the scene at the party with the rich children and their gifts.

26. D) Sunlight filtering through closed shutters]

Explanation: The phrase that represents the bright light creeping through the shutters that woke up the children is the fourth phrase, which depicts sunlight filtering through closed shutters. In the passage, it is mentioned that a light as bright as day crept through the shutters, indicating that it was sunlight. Therefore, the fourth phrase best represents the described scene in the text.

Option A, A sun shining brightly in the sky, is incorrect because the passage does not mention a sun shining brightly in the sky. The source of the light in the story is sunlight filtering through the shutters, not direct sunlight from the sky. Option B, Moonlight casting a glow on the trees, is incorrect because the passage does not mention moonlight. It specifically refers to a light as bright as day, which implies it is sunlight, not moonlight. Option C, A lamp turned on in a dark room, is incorrect because the passage mentions the lamp upon the table lighting again by itself, not a lamp turned on in a dark room. The bright light is attributed to the sunlight, not a lamp.

www.math-knots.com | www.a4ace.com

27. C) Brightly lit house with decorations and a Christmas tree]

Explanation: The phrase that represents the scene described when the children saw the lights of the party at the rich children's house is the third sentence, which depicts a brightly lit house with decorations and a Christmas tree. In the passage, Tyltyl notices the bright lights coming from the rich children's house, which he refers to as a party. The lights and the mention of a Christmas tree indicate a festive setting with decorations. Therefore, the third phrase best represents the described scene in the text.

Option A, Children opening presents under a Christmas tree, is incorrect because the passage does not describe the children in the rich children's house opening presents. The focus is on the lights and the Christmas tree, not the act of opening presents. Option B, Children dancing and playing at a birthday party, is incorrect because the passage does not mention children dancing and playing at the party. The focus is on the observation of the lights and the Christmas tree, not on the activities of the children at the party. Option D, Children sleeping peacefully in their beds, is incorrect because the passage describes the children waking up and seeing the lights of the party. The scene of children sleeping peacefully in their beds does not match the described situation.

SUBMARINES: EXPLORING THE DEEP SEA

28. C) Paragraph 4

Explanation: The importance of lights and special equipment in submarines is mentioned in Paragraph 4. It states that submarines have special equipment and lights to help the crew see and explore the dark and cold underwater environment. This indicates the significance of lights and special equipment in enabling the crew to navigate and conduct their exploration in the deep sea. Therefore, option C is the correct answer.

Option A, Paragraph 1, is incorrect because it describes the hull and periscope of the submarine, but it does not mention lights or special equipment. Option B, Paragraph 2, is incorrect because it talks about the propellers and movement of the submarine, but it does not mention lights or special equipment. Option D, Paragraph 5, is incorrect because it provides a concluding statement about the overall fascination and exploration of submarines, but it does not specifically mention lights or special equipment.

29. C) Hull

Explanation: The top part of a submarine is called the hull. In the passage, it is mentioned that the hull of a submarine is made of strong metal and helps to keep the water out, ensuring the safety and dryness of everyone inside. Therefore, option C is the correct answer.

Option A, "Propeller," is incorrect because the propeller is not the top part of a submarine. It is mentioned in the passage that submarines have propellers at the back, which are responsible for moving the submarine forward. Option B, "Periscope," is incorrect because the periscope is a long telescope-like device that sticks out of the water and allows the people inside the submarine to see what's happening above. It is not the top part of the submarine. Option D, "Telescope," is incorrect because a telescope is not the top part of a submarine. The periscope is described as being like a long telescope, but it is not the top part of the submarine itself.

30. **A) Control room**

Explanation: The section of a submarine that is responsible for steering and monitoring is the control room. In the passage, it is mentioned that the control room is where the captain and crew steer the submarine and make sure everything is working properly. Therefore, option A is the correct answer.

Option B, "Kitchen," is incorrect because the kitchen is the section where food is prepared, not where the submarine is steered and monitored. Option C, "Bedroom," is incorrect because the bedroom is where the crew rests, not where the submarine is steered and monitored. Option D, "Exercise room," is incorrect because the exercise room is the section where the crew can exercise, not where the submarine is steered and monitored.

31. **A) Control room**

The section of a submarine responsible for steering and monitoring is the control room (Option A). The section of a submarine responsible for steering and monitoring is the control room. In the control room, the captain and crew operate the submarine and make sure everything is working properly. They use instruments and controls to navigate the submarine through the water. The other choices, such as the kitchen, bedroom, and exercise room, are incorrect. The kitchen is where food is prepared, the bedroom is where the crew rests, and the exercise room is where they exercise. While these rooms are important for daily living on the submarine, they do not have the equipment or controls necessary for steering and monitoring the submarine's movements. Only the control room is specifically designed for that purpose.

32. **D) lights**

Submarines have special lights that shine in the deep sea and help the crew see what's around them. The lights are like little lamps that brighten up the dark ocean. They make it easier for the crew to explore and discover the underwater world.

The other choices, A) periscope, B) telescope, and C) propeller, are incorrect because they do not directly help the crew see in the dark underwater. A periscope is a long telescope-like device that sticks out of the water to let the crew see what's happening above the surface, not underwater in the dark. A telescope is an optical instrument used to see things that are far away, such as stars or objects on land. It is not used to see underwater. A propeller is a device that helps move the submarine forward by pushing water backward, but it does not assist with seeing in the dark.

Therefore, the correct answer is D) lights because they are specifically designed to provide visibility in the dark underwater environment.

33. **D) To see above the water surface**

The purpose of a periscope on a submarine is D) to see above the water surface. A periscope is like a long telescope that sticks out of the water and helps the crew see what's happening above. It has mirrors inside that reflect the view from above the water down into the submarine, allowing the crew to look around without coming up to the surface. This is important for the crew to stay hidden and be aware of their surroundings. The other choices, A) to keep the water out, B) to carry supplies, and C) to steer the submarine, are incorrect because they do not describe the purpose of a periscope.

A periscope does not keep the water out of the submarine. The hull, which is the top part of the submarine, is responsible for keeping the water out. Carrying supplies is not the primary purpose of a periscope. It is used for observation and gathering information rather than transportation. Steering the submarine is done through other controls and systems within the control room, not through the periscope.

Therefore, the correct answer is D) to see above the water surface because a periscope allows the crew to have a view of what's happening outside the submarine without having to emerge from underwater.

34. C) Having bedrooms

Living in a submarine is similar to living in a home because submarines have bedrooms (C) where the crew members can rest. In a home, we also have bedrooms where we sleep and have our own personal space. While a control room (A) is important for operating the submarine, it is not directly related to the similarity of living in a submarine to living in a home. A periscope (B) is a unique feature of a submarine that allows people inside to see above the water, but it is not directly related to the living conditions inside the submarine. Propellers (D) are part of the submarine's propulsion system and are necessary for moving the submarine underwater, but they do not contribute to the similarity of living in a submarine to living in a home. Thus, the correct answer is C) Having bedrooms.

35. C) Oceans

Submarines can explore the oceans with their special equipment and lights. Oceans are big bodies of water, like the sea, and submarines are like special boats that can go underwater. They have lights and tools to help them see and explore underwater. The other choices, mountains, deserts, and forests, are not right because submarines cannot go to those places. Mountains are very tall and rocky, deserts are dry and sandy, and forests have lots of trees. Submarines are made to go in the water, so they can only explore the oceans with their special equipment and lights. That's where they can find exciting things and discover the secrets of the deep sea!

36. C) Supplies and equipment

Submarines can carry supplies and equipment for scientific research or military missions. This means they can bring important things like tools, instruments, and materials that scientists or the military need for their work. Submarines are not used to carry food and water because they have their own supplies inside. They are also not used to carry animals and plants because submarines are not suitable environments for them to live in. Submarines are not meant for carrying passengers and tourists either, as they are specialized vehicles used for specific purposes like exploring the ocean depths. So, the correct answer is C) Supplies and equipment.

Explanation:

Submarines are like special ships that can go underwater. They are used for scientific research or military missions. When submarines are underwater, they can carry supplies and equipment that scientists or the military need for their work. These supplies and equipment can include tools, instruments, and materials that are important for their missions. Submarines are not used to carry food and water because they have their own supplies inside. They are also not used to carry animals and plants because submarines are not suitable

environments for them to live in. Submarines are not meant for carrying passengers and tourists either, as they are specialized vehicles used for specific purposes like exploring the ocean depths. So, the correct answer is C) Supplies and equipment.

THE TALE OF SQUIRREL NUTKIN – BY BEATRIX POTTER

37. **A) Paragraph 1.**

In the story, Nutkin is introduced as a little red squirrel with a tail. The paragraph tells us that the tale is about Nutkin, the little red squirrel.

The other choices are incorrect because they do not mention Nutkin specifically.

Choice B) Paragraph 2 introduces Nutkin's brother, Twinkleberry, and his cousins, but it doesn't mention Nutkin himself. Choice C) Paragraph 3 introduces Old Brown, the owl who lives in the hollow oak-tree, but it doesn't mention Nutkin. Choice D) Paragraph 4 talks about Nutkin and the other little squirrels coming out of the wood to gather nuts, but it doesn't explicitly introduce Nutkin as a character. Only Paragraph 1 directly states that the story is about a little red squirrel named Nutkin, making it the correct choice.

38. **A) Twinkleberry.**

In Paragraph 2, it is mentioned that Nutkin had a brother called Twinkleberry. Therefore, Twinkleberry is the name of Nutkin's brother. The other choices are incorrect:

B) Old Brown is the name of the owl who lives in the hollow oak tree. C) Nutkin is the name of the little red squirrel himself. D) Mr. Brown is a polite way the squirrels address the owl, Old Brown.

39. **B) Sticks.**

In Paragraph 5, it is mentioned that the squirrels made little rafts out of twigs. Therefore, the squirrels used sticks to make their rafts. The other choices are incorrect:

A) Leaves are not mentioned as being used to make rafts. C) Rocks are not mentioned as being used to make rafts. D) Feathers are not mentioned as being used to make rafts.

40. **B) Impertinently.**

Nutkin behaved impertinently towards Old Brown. In Paragraph 9, it is stated that Nutkin was excessively impertinent in his manners. He bobbed up and down, singing a riddle and being disrespectful.

The other choices are incorrect because they do not accurately describe Nutkin's behavior towards Old Brown:

A) Respectfully is incorrect because Nutkin's behavior was disrespectful and impertinent, not respectful. C) Shyly is incorrect because Nutkin's behavior was bold and cheeky, not shy. D) Gratefully is incorrect because Nutkin did not show gratitude towards Old Brown; instead, he displayed impertinence.

41. **C) Moles.**

The squirrels brought a fine fat mole to Old Brown the second time. In Paragraph 12, it is mentioned that Twinkleberry and the other squirrels brought a mole and laid it on the stone in front of Old Brown's doorway. Therefore, moles were the offering they brought to Old Brown on their second visit. The other choices are incorrect:

A) Nuts were the items the squirrels gathered from Owl Island, not the offering they brought to Old Brown. B) Mice were the offering the squirrels brought on their first visit, not the second. D) Acorns are not mentioned as being brought to Old Brown in the story.

42. **B) Paragraph 5.**

In Paragraph 5, it is described how the squirrels made little rafts out of twigs and paddled away over the water to Owl Island to gather nuts. This paragraph specifically mentions the activity of making rafts and gathering nuts. The other choices are incorrect:

A) Paragraph 4 talks about Nutkin, Twinkleberry, and the other little squirrels coming out of the wood and down to the edge of the lake, but it does not mention the specific activity of making rafts and gathering nuts. C) Paragraph 6 mentions the squirrels having little sacks and large oars, but it does not describe the activity of making rafts and gathering nuts. D) Paragraph 7 talks about the squirrels taking an offering of three fat mice for Old Brown, but it does not describe the activity of making rafts and gathering nuts.

43. **B) very good of its kind.**

In this context, 'fine' is used to describe the quality or condition of the mole. It implies that the mole is excellent or of high quality. The other choices are incorrect:

A) The meaning of "very thin or narrow" does not fit the description of the mole. C) The meaning of "a sum of money to be paid as money" is unrelated to the sentence. D) The meaning of "made of small particles" is unrelated to the sentence.

IKTOMI AND THE DUCKS – ZITKALA-SA

44. **A) Paragraph 1.**

In Paragraph 1, Iktomi's appearance is described in detail, including his clothing and physical features. It mentions his brown deerskin leggings with fringes, tiny beaded moccasins, long black hair, red bands, braids, and how they hang over his ears and shoulders. This paragraph provides a visual description of Iktomi's appearance. The other choices are incorrect:

B) Paragraph 2 describes Iktomi's dress and how he dresses like a real Dakota brave, but it does not provide a detailed physical description. C) Paragraph 3 talks about Iktomi's mischievous nature and his preference for spreading snares, but it does not describe his appearance. D) Paragraph 4 talks about Iktomi's conceit and how he thinks he is brighter than others, but it does not describe his appearance.

45. **C) Spread traps and snares.**

In Paragraph 3, it is mentioned that Iktomi prefers to spread a snare rather than to earn the smallest thing with honest hunting. This implies that Iktomi's preference is to set traps and snares rather than engaging in honest hunting to obtain things. The other choices are incorrect:

A) The passage does not mention that Iktomi prefers to earn things with honest hunting. B) The passage states that no one helps Iktomi when he is in trouble, suggesting that he does not actively help others in need. D) While it is mentioned that Iktomi laughs with a wide-open mouth when others are caught in traps, this is not specifically mentioned as his preference but rather as a reaction to others being caught.

46. **B) Because he is a naughty fairy.**

In Paragraph 5, it is stated that Iktomi cannot find a single friend and that no one helps him when he is in trouble. The passage implies that his mischievous and naughty nature is the reason why he doesn't receive help or have friends. His vain words, heartless laughter, and mischief make people sick and tired of him, leading to his isolation and lack of support. The other choices are incorrect:

A) While it is mentioned that Iktomi has no friends, the reason for that is his naughty behavior rather than simply not having friends. C) While it is stated that Iktomi is conceited, it is not explicitly mentioned as the reason why no one helps him when he is in trouble. D) The fact that Iktomi lives alone in a wigwam is mentioned, but it is not given as the reason why no one helps him when he is in trouble.

47. **C) They grow sick and tired of it.**

In Paragraph 5, it is mentioned that people who come to admire Iktomi's appearance and clothing, such as his beaded jacket and fringed leggings, soon go away sick and tired of his vain words and heartless laughter. This indicates that people do not have a positive reaction to Iktomi's vanity and heartless laughter. Instead, they become weary or fatigued by it. The other choices are incorrect:

A) The passage does not indicate that people admire Iktomi's vanity and heartless laughter. B) While it is not explicitly stated whether people find it amusing or not, the phrase "sick and tired" suggests a negative response rather than finding it amusing. D) The passage does not mention that people try to imitate Iktomi's vanity and heartless laughter.

48. **C) Because he has no friends.**

In the passage, it is mentioned in Paragraph 5 that Iktomi cannot find a single friend and that no one really loves him. As a result, he lives alone in a cone-shaped wigwam on the plain. The implication is that his lack of companionship and friendship is the reason why he lives alone. The other choices are incorrect:

A) While Iktomi may live alone in solitude, the passage does not indicate that he enjoys it or actively seeks solitude as a preference. B) While it is mentioned that people grow tired of Iktomi's vanity and heartless laughter, the passage does not explicitly state that Iktomi doesn't like people. D) The passage does not provide information to suggest that Iktomi prefers the wigwam over other homes.

49. B) Iktomi's behavior causes people to avoid him.

The passage clearly indicates that Iktomi's behavior, which includes his vanity, heartless laughter, and mischief, leads people to grow sick and tired of him. It states that no one helps him when he is in trouble and

that he cannot find a single friend. These details suggest that Iktomi's behavior has a negative effect on others, causing them to avoid him rather than admire or imitate him. The other choices are incorrect:

A) The passage does not mention that Iktomi's behavior makes people admire him. C) The passage does not suggest that Iktomi's behavior makes people want to imitate him. D) The passage clearly states that people grow sick and tired of Iktomi, indicating that his behavior does have an effect on others.

50. D) Basins.

Both words have a similar ending sound, with the "-ins" rhyming with each other. The other choices do not rhyme with "moccasins":

A) "Deerskin" does not rhyme with "moccasins."

B) "Mischief" does not rhyme with "moccasins."

C) "Parted" does not rhyme with "moccasins."

THE OWL AND THE GRASSHOPPER

1. D. Bugs and beetles, frogs, and mice

Explanation: Owls hunt for bugs and beetles, as well as frogs and mice. These are the creatures they like to eat. The story mentions, "she begins her hunt for the bugs and beetles, frogs and mice she likes so well to eat." Choice A (Bugs) is not the complete answer because owls hunt for more than just bugs. Choice C (Frogs and mice) is also not the complete answer because owls also hunt for bugs and beetles. Choice B (Bugs and beetles) is not the complete answer because it leaves out the fact that owls also hunt for frogs and mice. Therefore, the correct answer is D, which includes all the animals that owls hunt for.

2. C. Old owl

Explanation: The line "Get away from here, sir" was said by the Old owl. In the story, the Old owl is disturbed by the Grasshopper's raspy song while she is trying to sleep during the day, and she pops her head out of her tree den to address the Grasshopper. Choice A (Grasshopper) is incorrect because the Grasshopper is the one singing and interacting with the Old owl. Choice B (Frog) is incorrect because there is no mention of a frog in this particular part of the story. Choice D (None of them) is incorrect because the Old owl is indeed the one who said this line to the Grasshopper. Therefore, the correct answer is C, the Old owl.

3. C. Olympus

Explanation: The wonderful wine mentioned in the story was sent from Olympus. The Old owl tells the Grasshopper that she has this special wine from Olympus, which is said to be the same wine that Apollo drinks before he sings to the high gods. Choice A (Apollo) is incorrect because Apollo is associated with drinking the wine, but he did not send it. Choice B (A friend) is not mentioned in the story as the sender of the wine. Choice D (Jupiter) is also not mentioned as the sender. Therefore, the correct answer is C, Olympus.

4. A. To offer him a drink

Explanation: The owl called the grasshopper to her den to offer him a drink. In the story, the old owl uses flattery to lure the grasshopper closer by telling him that she has a wonderful wine from Olympus that will make him sing like Apollo. She invites him to taste the delicious drink with her. Choices B (To teach him a lesson), C (To enjoy his singing), and D (To have company) are not the primary reasons mentioned in the story for the owl's actions. The owl's intention was to deceive the grasshopper by offering him the drink and then taking advantage of his trust. Therefore, the correct answer is A, to offer him a drink.

5. D: A and B

Explanation: The old owl became cross and hard because she had grown old and also because someone disturbed her slumber. The story mentions that as she grew older, she became very cross and hard to please, especially if anything disturbed her daily slumbers. Both choices A (Because she had grown old) and B (Someone disturbed her slumber) are mentioned in the story as reasons for the old owl's behavior. Choice C (She couldn't see clearly) is not mentioned as a reason for her becoming cross and hard. Therefore, the correct answer is D, A and B.

6. C. Sleep

Explanation: The word 'slumber' means sleep. In the story, it is mentioned that the old owl became cross and hard to please, especially if anything disturbed her daily slumbers, which refers to her sleep. Choice A (Reading), B (Roar), and D (Hunt) do not accurately capture the meaning of the word 'slumber' as used in the context of the story. Therefore, the correct answer is C, sleep.

www.math-knots.com | www.a4ace.com

7. A. Impudently

Explanation: The synonym of "saucily" is "impudently." In the story, the Grasshopper answered "saucily" when he responded to the Old owl, showing a disrespectful and bold attitude. Choice B (Humbly), C (Modestly), and D (Politely) are not synonyms of "saucily" as they convey different manners of behavior. Therefore, the correct answer is A, impudently.

8. D. All of the above

Explanation: The best description of the moral of the story is encompassed by all three options: A) "All that glitters is not gold," B) "Flattery is not a proof of true admiration," and C) "Don't let your enemy's flattery catch you unaware." The story teaches us the dangers of being deceived by flattering words, not underestimating the true intentions of others, and being cautious of potential enemies. Therefore, the correct answer is D, all of the above.

OLD SULTAN

9. D. Being killed by the shepherd

Explanation: The main concern for Sultan in the story is the fear of being killed by the shepherd. The story begins with the shepherd discussing his intention to shoot old Sultan, who has become old and toothless, stating that he is of no use anymore. Sultan overhears this conversation and becomes frightened that his master plans to kill him. This fear drives the actions that follow in the story, including seeking advice from the wolf and eventually saving the shepherd's child from the wolf's plan. The other options (A, B, and C) are not the central concern of Sultan in the story; his main worry revolves around his own survival and avoiding being killed by his master.

10. A. To fool the shepherd and his wife

Explanation: Sultan pretends to watch the shepherd's child to fool the shepherd and his wife into thinking that he is protecting the child from danger. The wolf advises Sultan to do this so that when the wolf attempts to carry away the child, Sultan can chase after him, make him drop the child, and then return the child to the shepherd and his wife. This plan is meant to make Sultan appear as a hero and earn the gratitude of his master and mistress, thereby securing his livelihood and safety. The other options (B, C, and D) do not accurately capture the purpose of Sultan's actions in pretending to watch the child.

11. A. He gets hit with a cudgel

Explanation: When the wolf tries to get a sheep from the shepherd's farm, he gets hit with a cudgel by Sultan. The story mentions that Sultan had informed his master about the wolf's intentions, and his master lays in wait for the wolf behind the barn door. When the wolf comes to carry away a sheep, Sultan's master strikes the wolf with a cudgel, giving him a sound beating. This event illustrates that the shepherd is protective of his sheep and takes action to defend them from predators like the wolf. The other options (B, C, and D) are not consistent with the events in the story.

12. B. Because it is a three-legged cat

Explanation: The cat has to limp because it is a three-legged cat. In the story, Sultan, the faithful dog, takes the shepherd's old three-legged cat as his second when challenged to a fight by the wolf. As they approach

the wolf and wild boar, the cat limps along with some trouble due to having only three legs. This limp is mistaken by the wolf and boar as a deliberate action, making them believe that the cat is carrying a sword for Sultan to fight with. The other choices, A (Because it is following Sultan's lead), C (Because it is laughing at the situation), and D (Because it is injured during the fight), are not accurate explanations for the cat's limp in the context of the story. Therefore, the correct answer is B, because it is a three-legged cat.

13. C. They mistake the cat's tail and limping for weapons

Explanation: The wolf and the wild boar hide from Sultan and the cat because they mistake the cat's tail standing straight in the air and her limping for weapons that Sultan and the cat might be carrying. In the story, as Sultan and the cat approach the wolf and the boar, the wolf and boar see the cat's tail and believe that she is carrying a sword for Sultan to fight with. Additionally, they think that every time the cat limps, she is picking up a stone to throw at them. This misunderstanding leads the wolf to climb a tree and the boar to hide behind a bush, as they fear facing these supposed threats. The other choices, A (They want to surprise Sultan and the cat), B (They are waiting for a better opportunity to attack), and D (They are afraid of Sultan's barking), do not accurately describe the wolf and boar's actions and motivations in the context of the story. Therefore, the correct answer is C, they mistake the cat's tail and limping for weapons.

14. C. The wolf's location

Explanation: The boar reveals the wolf's location when the cat attacks its ear. In the story, when the cat, seeing something move, mistakes the boar's ear for a mouse and attacks it by biting and scratching, the boar grunts and runs away. As the boar flees, it shouts out, "Look up in the tree, there sits the one who is to blame." This statement indicates that the boar is revealing the wolf's location, who had climbed up into the tree to avoid the confrontation with Sultan and the cat. The other choices (A, B, and D) are not accurate descriptions of what the boar reveals when the cat attacks its ear in the context of the story. Therefore, the correct answer is C, the wolf's location.

15. D. Faithfulness and loyalty

Explanation: The characteristics of Sultan that are most valued by the shepherd and his wife are his faithfulness and loyalty. In the story, Sultan has served the shepherd and his wife well for many years, and his loyalty to them is evident in his actions. When the shepherd plans to shoot Sultan, his wife argues that Sultan deserves to live due to his faithful service. Additionally, Sultan's act of saving the shepherd's child from the wolf further demonstrates his loyalty and devotion. The other choices (A, B, and C) do not accurately capture the main qualities that the shepherd and his wife value in Sultan in the context of the story. Therefore, the correct answer is D, faithfulness, and loyalty.

16. A. He is loyal to his master

Explanation: Sultan refuses to help the wolf steal from the shepherd's flock because he is loyal to his master. In the story, Sultan is determined to protect the shepherd's sheep and remain true to his master. He has already informed his master about the wolf's intention to steal from the flock, and he takes action to prevent it. This loyalty and devotion to his master's well-being and property guide his decision to resist the wolf's request for help. The other choices (B, C, and D) do not accurately capture the main reason for Sultan's refusal in the context of the story. Therefore, the correct answer is A, he is loyal to his master.

www.math-knots.com | www.a4ace.com

17. B. Because Sultan foiled the wolf's plan

Explanation: The wolf calls Sultan 'an old rogue' because Sultan foiled the wolf's plan to steal from the shepherd's flock. In the story, Sultan had informed his master about the wolf's intention to steal sheep, and his master set a trap to catch the wolf. When the wolf attempts to carry out the theft, Sultan is waiting behind the barn door and hits the wolf with a cudgel, preventing the theft. The wolf's frustration and anger at having his plan thwarted lead him to call Sultan 'an old rogue.' The other choices (A, C, and D) do not accurately capture the reason for the wolf's name-calling in the context of the story.

Therefore, the correct answer is B because Sultan foiled the wolf's plan.

THE QUARREL OF THE QUAILS

18. D. Their leader

Explanation: The wisest of all the quails in the forest was their leader. In the story, it is mentioned that the leader of the quails was the one who came up with the plan to outsmart the fowler and save the quails from being caught. The other options (A, B, and C) do not accurately describe the wisest quail's identity in the context of the story. Therefore, the correct answer is D, their leader.

19. A. By throwing a net over them

Explanation: The Fowler caught the quails by throwing a net over them. In the story, it is mentioned that the fowler listened to the note of the leader calling the quails day after day. He learned to mimic the leader's call, and when the quails crowded together upon hearing the call, he threw his net over them, capturing them to be sold. The other options (B, C, and D) do not accurately describe the method used by the fowler to catch the quails in the context of the story. Therefore, the correct answer is A, by throwing a net over them.

20. C. Put their heads through the holes in the net and fly away with it

Explanation: The plan suggested by the quail leader to avoid getting caught by the fowler was to put their heads through the holes in the net and fly away with it. The leader of the quails realized that the fowler was capturing them with his net, so he came up with a clever plan to escape. He advised the quails that the next time the fowler threw a net over them, each of them should put their heads through one of the little holes in the net. Then, together, they should fly away to the nearest thorn bush, leaving the net behind and freeing themselves. The other options (A, B, and D) are not accurate descriptions of the plan suggested by the quail leader in the context of the story. Therefore, the correct answer is C, put their heads through the holes in the net and fly away with it.

21. D. Left it on a thorn-bush

Explanation: After flying away with the net, the quails left it on a thorn-bush. The quail leader's plan was for the quails to escape by flying with the net to the nearest thorn bush and leaving it there. This would allow them to free themselves from the net and prevent the fowler from capturing them. The other options (A, B, and C) are not accurate descriptions of what the quails did with the net in the context of the story. Therefore, the correct answer is D, left it on a thorn-bush.

22. C. They couldn't decide who should lift the net

Explanation: When fowler threw the net over the quarreling quails, they couldn't decide who should lift the net. In the story, the quails had taken sides in a quarrel and were arguing about lifting the net. One side said,

"Now, you lift the net," and the other side said, "Lift it yourself." The quails were unable to come to an agreement or take coordinated action, which ultimately led to their capture by the fowler. The other options (A, B, and D) are not accurate descriptions of the quails' reaction when the net was thrown over them in the context of the story. Therefore, the correct answer is C, they couldn't decide who should lift the net.

23. B. They were too busy quarreling to fly away

Explanation: The Fowler said the quails were easy to catch after they started arguing because they were too busy quarreling to fly away. In the story, the quails' argument and inability to work together allowed the Fowler to capture them easily. Instead of following the wise leader's plan to lift the net and fly away to the thorn bush, the quails were caught up in their dispute, providing the Fowler with an opportunity to capture them while they were distracted. The other options (A, C, and D) do not accurately describe why the fowler found the quails easy to catch in the context of the story. Therefore, the correct answer is B, they were too busy quarreling to fly away.

24. D. to descend from or as if from the air and come to rest

Explanation: In the context of the passage, the term 'alighting' refers to the action of descending from the air and coming to rest. This meaning is consistent with the way it is used when mentioning that one of the quails "alighted on their feeding ground." The other options (A, B, and C) do not accurately capture the meaning of 'alighting' as used in the passage. Therefore, the correct answer is D, to descend from or as if from the air and come to rest.

25. C. Farthest

Explanation: In the context of the sentence, "-est" is used to indicate the superlative form, which means the highest degree of comparison. In this case, "nearest" means the closest or most close. Similarly, in the word "farthest," the "-est" ending indicates the highest degree of distance, meaning the most distant or most far. The other options (A, B, and D) do not accurately capture the meaning of "-est" as used in the sentence. Therefore, the correct answer is C, farthest.

26. C. Unity is strength

Explanation: The moral of the story is that unity is strength. The story illustrates how the quails were able to successfully escape the fowler's trap and outsmart him when they worked together and followed their wise leader's plan. When they quarreled and couldn't cooperate, they became vulnerable and were easily captured. This conveys the message that when individuals unite and work together towards a common goal, they are stronger and more likely to succeed. The other options (A, B, and D) do not accurately capture the main lesson or moral of the story. Therefore, the correct answer is C, unity is strength.

CASABIANCA

27. A. The air was filled with black smoke.

Explanation: In the passage, it is mentioned that during the naval battle, the air was filled with black smoke. The description of the battle includes the roar of big guns, broken masts, and pieces of timber strewn in the water due to cannonballs. This indicates that the battle resulted in heavy smoke and chaos, making the correct answer option A, "The air was filled with black smoke." The other options (B, C, and D) do not accurately describe the condition of the air as portrayed in the passage.

28. C. The flames were spreading rapidly.

Explanation: Staying on board the burning ship was dangerous because the flames were spreading rapidly. In the passage, it is mentioned that the flagship had taken fire, and the flames were breaking out from below, engulfing the deck and the masts. The fire was described as leaping up the masts, blazing the sails, and surrounding the young Ca-sa-bi-an′ca. This indicates that the fire was spreading quickly, making it hazardous to remain on the burning ship. The other options (A, B, and D) do not accurately describe the immediate danger caused by the fire as portrayed in the passage.

29. a. He trusted in his father's word and believed he would be told to go.

Explanation: Young Ca-sa-bi-an′ca stayed on the burning ship because he trusted in his father's word and believed that his father would eventually tell him to go. In the passage, it is mentioned that Ca-sa-bi-an′ca's father had instructed him to stand on the deck and that he had been taught always to obey his father's commands. Even when the flames were almost all around him and others were urging him to leave, Ca-sa-bi-an′ca remained steadfast, believing that his father's order would come at the right time. The other options (B, C, and D) do not accurately capture the motivation behind Ca-sa-bi-an′ca's decision to stay on the burning ship as portrayed in the passage.

30. B. His father had been killed at the beginning of the fight.

Explanation: Young Ca-sa-bi-an′ca could not hear his father because his father had been killed at the beginning of the fight. In the passage, it is revealed that Ca-sa-bi-an′ca was not aware that his father was lying in the burning cabin below, and a cannonball had struck his father dead at the very beginning of the battle. Despite calling out to his father and listening for his answer, Ca-sa-bi-an′ca did not realize that his father was no longer able to respond. The other options (A, C, and D) do not accurately explain why Ca-sa-bi-an′ca could not hear his father as portrayed in the passage.

31. D. His father's voice faintly through the scorching air.

Explanation: Young Ca-sa-bi-an′ca thought he heard his father's voice faintly through the scorching air. In the passage, Ca-sa-bi-an′ca, surrounded by flames and chaos, desperately listened for his father's response to his questions and calls. He believed that he heard his father's voice coming faintly to him through the scorching air, above the noise of the battle, the flames, and the crashing of the falling spars. This indicates that Ca-sa-bi-an′ca perceived his father's voice, even though his father had actually been killed earlier in the battle. The other options (A, B, and C) do not accurately describe what Ca-sa-bi-an′ca thought he heard as portrayed in the passage.

32. B. An explosion of powder.

Explanation: The ultimate event that brought an end to Casabianca's story was an explosion of powder. In the passage, it is mentioned that there was powder in the hold of the burning ship. Despite Ca-sa-bi-an′ca's loyalty and determination to stay on board, hoping for his father's command to leave, the presence of powder in the hold led to a tragic explosion. The passage describes a great flash of light, clouds of smoke shooting upward, and a tremendous boom, indicating a massive explosion. This event resulted in the ship's destruction and the tragic end of Ca-sa-bi-an′ca's story. The other options (A, C, and D) do not accurately represent the final event that ended Casabianca's story as portrayed in the passage.

         www.math-knots.com | www.a4ace.com

33. C. It was no longer visible.

Explanation: After the explosion of powder, the blazing ship was no longer visible. In the passage, it is described that a great flash of light filled the air, followed by clouds of smoke shooting quickly upward to the sky. The tremendous boom and the subsequent effects of the explosion caused the ship to disappear from the sight. The ship was consumed by the explosion and the resulting chaos, leading to its disappearance. The other options (A, B, and D) do not accurately describe the fate of the blazing ship as portrayed in the passage.

34. B. There was a lot of smoke in the air.

Explanation: The phrase "The sky is black." most likely implies that there was a lot of smoke in the air. In the passage, it is described that after the explosion, a great flash of light filled the air, followed by clouds of smoke shooting quickly upward to the sky. The description of the sky being black is a result of the smoke and chaos caused by the explosion. This option best captures the meaning of the phrase in the context of the passage. The other options (A, C, and D) do not accurately convey the implied meaning of the phrase as portrayed in the passage.

ELECTRICITY

35. B. Amber

Explanation: The Latin word 'electricity' is said to have come from the name the Latins gave to amber, which is 'electrum.' The text mentions that our word "electricity" appears to be derived from the name the Latins gave to amber. Amber is known to have electrical properties, as mentioned earlier in the text, and it was one of the substances with which the ancients were acquainted in terms of its electrical properties. The other choices (A, C, and D) are not mentioned in relation to the origin of the word "electricity" in the text.

36. C. Thalis

Explanation: As mentioned in the text, the Miletine philosophers, including Thalis, believed that the attractive power of the magnet and amber was due to animation by a vital principle. The text states, "Even before Pliny, however, as early as the days of Thalis, who lived near six hundred years anterior to the Roman historian, the Miletine philosophers ascribed the attractive power of the magnet and of amber to animation by a vital principle." The other choices (A, B, and D) are not associated with this belief about the magnet and amber.

37. A. mysterious or specialized knowledge, language, or information accessible or possessed only by the initiate

Explanation: In the given sentence, "arcana" refers to mysterious or specialized knowledge or information that is not widely understood and is accessible only to those who are initiated or knowledgeable in a particular field. The sentence implies that electricity, like other aspects of nature, remains largely unknown and mysterious to most people. The other choices (B, C, and D) do not accurately capture the meaning of "arcana" as used in this context.

38. D. "It has been asserted that the ancients knew how to collect the electrical fire in the atmosphere"
Explanation: Among the given options, sentence d does not directly indicate that experimenting with electricity can be life-threatening. The other options (A, B, and C) clearly mention incidents or accidents where individuals lost their lives due to experiments involving electricity, highlighting the potential dangers associated with such experiments.

39. A. Anterior
Explanation: The meanings provided match the word "anterior" from the passage. "Anterior" means situated before or toward the front or head, which fits all the provided meanings. The other choices are incorrect because they do not align with these meanings. "Conjectural" means based on guesswork or speculation, "appellation" means a name or title, and "acquainted" means familiar with or knowledgeable about something.

40. C. Hawkesbee, Grey, Muschenbrook
Explanation: The correct answer is C. Hawkesbee, Grey, Muschenbrook, along with other notable figures like Doctors Franklin and Priestly, Bishop Watson, and Mr. Cavendish, were some of the eminent philosophers who cultivated the science of electricity in the last century. Choices A, B, and D do not accurately list the philosophers mentioned in the passage.

41. a. When were the first discoveries related to electricity by Dr W. Gilbert?
Explanation: The correct answer is A. The fourth paragraph provides information about the first discoveries related to electricity, which were made by Dr. W. Gilbert and published in the year 1660 in a book titled "De Magneto." The other choices are not directly addressed in the fourth paragraph.

42. C. Royal Society of England
Explanation: The correct answer is C. Many eminent philosophers in England, including Doctors Franklin, Priestly, and Mr. Cavendish, belonged to the Royal Society of England. This information is mentioned in the passage. The other choices are not associated with the philosophers mentioned.

SHAZADPUR

43. C. dense, dark mist
Explanation: In the dream, the entire city of Calcutta was shrouded in a dense and ominous mist. This mist obscured the visibility of the houses, creating an eerie atmosphere and an aura of mystery. The mist enveloped the surroundings, making it difficult to see and adding to the sense of foreboding. Through this thick, dark mist, the houses and streets of Calcutta became dimly visible, and strange occurrences seemed to unfold within its veil. The mist played a significant role in shaping the dream's unsettling and mysterious setting. The other choices do not accurately capture the atmospheric condition described in the dream.

44. A. Park Street
Explanation: In the dream, Tagore saw St. Xavier's College as he was going along Park Street in a hackney carriage. As he passed by the college, he noticed something unusual – the building was rapidly growing and becoming impossibly high within the enveloping haze of the mist. This unexpected transformation of St. Xavier's College contributed to the dream's sense of wonder and mystery. The other options are not accurate locations where Tagore saw the college in the dream.

45. C. make men grow

Explanation: In the dream, the magicians had the power to make men grow taller. Tagore described how the magician sprinkled some powder over the heads of some girls, and they promptly shot up in height. This ability to make people grow was one of the strange and extraordinary feats attributed to the magicians in the dream. The other options do not accurately represent the magical ability described in the dream.

46. A. powder

Explanation: In the dream, the magician sprinkled powder over the heads of the girls to make them grow taller. This magical powder had the effect of causing the girls to shoot up in height. The other options are not mentioned as being used by the magician in the dream.

47. D. "This is most extraordinary, —just like a dream!"

Explanation: In the dream, whenever Tagore encountered the magicians and witnessed their magical feats, he kept repeating the phrase, "This is most extraordinary, —just like a dream!" This indicates his amazement and disbelief at the surreal and fantastical events taking place around him. The other options do not accurately reflect Tagore's reaction to the dream.

48. B. because the cashier strongly objected to paying before the work was completed

Explanation: In the dream, when the magicians began to dismantle the house as a part of their magical performance, they demanded payment for their services. However, the cashier strongly objected, stating that payment should only be made after the work was completed. This objection led to the magicians getting upset and wild, as they wanted assurance of payment before continuing with the task. The other options do not accurately describe the reason for the magicians' reaction in the dream.

49. D. "We had better call upon God to help us!"

Explanation: In the dream, when faced with the unsettling and chaotic situation caused by the magicians' actions, the dreamer suggests to his eldest brother that they should call upon God to help them. This reflects the dreamer's recognition of the need for divine intervention to address the challenges presented by the magicians' activities. The other options do not accurately capture the dreamer's response and suggestion in the dream.

50. B. a thoroughly devilish business

Explanation: In the dream, the dreamer compares the appearance of the building and people inside to "a thoroughly devilish business." This comparison conveys the chaotic, unsettling, and sinister nature of the situation created by the magicians' actions, where the building is twisted and distorted, and people are mixed up in unnatural ways. The dreamer's choice of words reflects the eerie and malevolent atmosphere of the dream. The other options do not accurately capture the dreamer's description of the scene.

Kaa's Hunting

1. B) The Law of the Jungle and how to communicate with various creatures.
In the passage, it is mentioned that Baloo and Bagheera taught Mowgli the Law of the Jungle, which includes how to speak to different animals like snakes, birds, and other beasts. This knowledge allowed Mowgli to communicate with various creatures and ask for permission not to be harmed by them. The other options are not explicitly mentioned in the passage: A) There is no mention of teaching Mowgli to speak to wolves;
C) While survival and hunting skills might be implied, they are not explicitly stated as the main focus of the teachings;
D) There is no mention of Baloo and Bagheera training Mowgli to become a ruler.

2. B) Because Mowgli disobeyed him and went against the Law of the Jungle.
Baloo became angry because Mowgli didn't follow the rules of the jungle, which is called the Law of the Jungle. Mowgli played with the Bandar-log instead of learning important things from Baloo and Bagheera. This made Baloo upset because Mowgli should have been listening and learning from his teachers. Other choices are incorrect because: A) The Bandar-log being disliked by the Jungle People is not the reason Baloo got angry. C) Mowgli becoming a leader for the Bandar-log is mentioned, but that's not why Baloo got angry. D) Mowgli not reciting the Law correctly is not the main reason for Baloo's anger; it's more about Mowgli not following the rules and listening to Baloo and Bagheera.

3. D) Kaa the Rock Python broke the wall holding him and helped him escape.
Mowgli was captured by the Monkey People and taken to the Cold Lair. When his friends Baloo and Bagheera learned about this, they asked Kaa the Rock Python for help. Kaa came to the rescue and broke the wall that was holding Mowgli. Kaa helped Mowgli escape from the Monkey People and the dangerous situation. Other choices are incorrect because: A) Mowgli didn't fight against the monkeys and escape on his own.
B) While Mowgli used a bird to call for help, it was Kaa who broke the wall to free him.
C) Mowgli convinced the snakes not to harm him, but this wasn't the main way he escaped the Cold Lair; Kaa's help was crucial.

4. B) Kaa put the Monkey People in a trance, allowing Mowgli and his friends to escape.
When the Monkey People had captured Mowgli and were attacking Baloo and Bagheera, Kaa the Rock Python arrived. Using his hissing and movement, Kaa put the Monkey People in a trance. This allowed Mowgli, Baloo, and Bagheera to escape from the Monkey People and the danger they posed. Other choices are incorrect because:
A) Kaa didn't attack the Monkey People directly; he used his abilities to put them in a trance.
C) While Kaa helped Mowgli escape, it wasn't by convincing the Monkey People to release him. D) Kaa did provide information about the Bandar-log's location, but putting them in a trance was his main action in this situation.

5. A) Bagheera cuffed Mowgli lightly, considering his young age.

Bagheera did punish Mowgli for his mischievousness, but he did so lightly by cuffing him. This is evident from the text: "The Law of the Jungle requires that Mowgli be cuffed for his mischievousness, but Bagheera cuffs him lightly, though it is quite a beating for a 7-year-old." The other choices are incorrect because: B) Bagheera did not give Mowgli a severe beating. C) There is no mention that Bagheera decided not to punish Mowgli.
D) There is no mention that Bagheera left the punishment to Baloo.

6. A) 1. behaving in a way that is slightly bad

In the context of the given passage, the word 'mischievous' is used to describe Mowgli's behavior, which is slightly bad or naughty. The passage mentions Mowgli being cuffed for his mischievousness, indicating that he was behaving in a slightly bad or naughty manner. The other meanings (B, C, D) involve causing more significant harm, damage, or trouble, which does not align with the description of Mowgli's behavior in this passage.

7. D) Paragraph 4

In paragraph 4 of the passage, it is mentioned that Kaa's hissing, and movement put the monkeys in a trance. This event occurs when Kaa arrives to assist Mowgli, Baloo, and Bagheera in dealing with the Monkey People.

The Bronze Ring

8. C) The gardeners lacked knowledge and experience

In the passage, it is mentioned that the gardeners of the King's garden were not able to make it yield flowers, fruits, grass, or trees because they did not understand their business. They lacked the necessary knowledge and experience to cultivate the garden effectively, which resulted in its lack of productivity.

9. C) To bring in a skilled gardener with a family history of gardening

The wise old man suggested to the King that he should send for a gardener whose father and grandfather have been gardeners before him. The old man believed that by bringing in a gardener with a family history of gardening, the King's garden would thrive and become full of green grass, flowers, and delicious fruit. This suggestion was based on the idea that generations of gardening knowledge and experience would lead to a successful garden.

10. C) He owed money to several people

The gardener hesitated to go and work for the King because he owed money to several people. When the messengers came to invite him to be the King's gardener, he said, "How can I go to the King, a poor wretch like me?" He was worried about his debts and thought he might not be able to leave his problems behind. The messengers assured him that it was not a problem, and they even promised to pay his

debts. This shows that his financial troubles were a big concern for him. The other choices are not the best answers because there is no clear evidence that he was afraid of the King's wrath, that he didn't want to leave his family, or that he didn't believe in his gardening abilities. The main reason for his hesitation was his money troubles.

11. C) He paid off the gardener's debts and offered new clothes

The King convinced the gardener to come and work for him by addressing his concerns. When the messengers invited the gardener to be the King's gardener, he hesitated because he owed money to several people and felt he was too poor to go. The messengers assured him by saying, "That is of no consequence," and they offered to pay off his debts and provide new clothes for him and his family. This gesture eased the gardener's financial worries and persuaded him to accept the offer to work for the King. The other choices are not the best answers because there is no evidence that the King promised to make him rich, threatened him with punishment, or offered the hand of the Princess in marriage. The key factor in convincing the gardener was addressing his financial concerns and providing the assistance with his debts.

12. B) The garden became full of green grass and flowers

The result of the gardener's work in the royal garden was that it transformed from being unproductive to becoming full of green grass and gay flowers. The wise old man's advice to bring in a skilled gardener with a family history of gardening proved successful. The gardener's expertise and care led to the flourishing of the garden, and it was no longer barren. The other choices are not the best answers because there is no evidence that the garden remained unproductive, turned into a dense forest, or was destroyed by pests. The passage clearly states that the gardener's efforts resulted in the garden thriving and being adorned with lush grass and vibrant flowers.

13. D) He wanted to see her settled and happy.

In the passage, the King considers marrying off his daughter because she is of a suitable age to take a husband. While the other options are possible considerations in other contexts, the passage does not provide evidence to suggest that the King's primary motivations were based on her age, forming alliances, or getting rid of her. The focus is more on the King's concern for his daughter's happiness and well-being in marriage.

14. D) He believed the gardener's son was not worthy of her.

The passage indicates that the King's initial reaction was a mixture of anger and disappointment upon hearing his daughter's declaration of love for the gardener's son. He wept, sighed, and declared that such a husband was not worthy of his daughter. This suggests that the King's anger was primarily rooted in his belief that the gardener's son was not a suitable match for the Princess based on social status and possibly other factors. The other options are not directly supported by the passage as the main reason for the King's anger in this context.

15. A) 1 - Result or Outcome

In the context of the passage, the word "consequence" refers to the result or outcome of the gardener's hesitation and decision to work for the King. The phrase "That is of no consequence" indicates that the gardener is expressing his concern about the potential results or outcomes of his decision to go and work for the King despite his financial situation. This choice aligns with the way the word is used in the passage. The other meanings (2, 3, and 4) do not fit the context as well and are not directly supported by the passage.

16. D) He wanted to decide who was more suitable for his daughter.

The passage mentions that the King consulted his ministers and followed their advice to send both suitors (the gardener's son and the minister's son) to a distant country. The purpose behind this action was to determine who would return first from the journey, which would help the King decide who was more suitable to marry his daughter. This choice aligns with the context of the passage, as the King wanted to make a decision about his daughter's marriage based on the outcome of the journey, showcasing the suitability and determination of the suitors. The other options do not accurately capture the King's intention as described in the passage.

The Life Cycle of a Butterfly

17. C) Larva

The second stage in a butterfly's life cycle is called the larva, also known as a caterpillar. During this stage, the caterpillar's main job is to eat and grow by munching on leaves and plants. The other choices are not the best answers because:

A) Pupa is the third stage, when the caterpillar changes inside a chrysalis;

B) Egg is the first stage, when tiny eggs are laid by the female butterfly;

D) Adult is the fourth stage, when the fully developed butterfly emerges from the chrysalis with expanded wings.

18. B) To eat and grow

The primary goal of a caterpillar during its life cycle is to eat and grow. Caterpillars have strong jaws that they use to munch on leaves and plants. As they eat, they grow rapidly and shed their skin multiple times to accommodate their increasing size. This helps them prepare for the next stage of their life cycle. The other choices are not the best answers because: A) Laying eggs is the goal of the adult female butterfly;

C) Transforming into a chrysalis is the next stage after the caterpillar has grown;

D) Flying and collecting nectar are activities of the adult butterfly.

19. B) Pupa (Chrysalis)

The stage of a butterfly's life cycle that involves the transformation from a caterpillar into a butterfly is the pupa or chrysalis stage. During this stage, the caterpillar attaches itself to a surface, sheds its outer skin, and undergoes a remarkable transformation inside the chrysalis. The caterpillar's body breaks

down into a soup-like substance and reforms into a butterfly. The other choices are not the best answers because:
A) The egg is the starting stage of the life cycle; C) The larva is the caterpillar stage;
D) The adult is the final stage after the butterfly emerges from the chrysalis.

20. C) By transferring pollen from one flower to another

Adult butterflies help plants reproduce by transferring pollen from one flower to another. When butterflies visit flowers to feed on nectar, pollen sticks to their bodies. As they move from flower to flower, they inadvertently transfer pollen, which contains the plant's male reproductive cells, to the female reproductive parts of the flowers. This process fertilizes the flowers and enables them to produce seeds and fruits. The other choices are not the best answers because: A) Laying eggs on plant leaves is part of the butterfly life cycle, not plant reproduction; B) Shedding their skin is a process that occurs during the caterpillar stage; D) Forming a chrysalis is also part of the butterfly life cycle, not plant reproduction.

21. B) Hidden or concealed from view

The word "camouflaged" is used to describe the appearance of butterfly eggs, indicating that they are hidden or concealed from view. When something is camouflaged, it is made to blend in with its surroundings to avoid being easily seen. In the context of butterfly eggs, being camouflaged helps protect them from predators. The other choices are not the best answers because: A) Attractive and colorful is not the meaning of "camouflaged"; Cc) Unusual or bizarre in appearance is not the meaning described in the context; D) Laid in large clusters refers to the arrangement of eggs, not their appearance.

22. A) The long, tube-like structure used by adult butterflies to collect nectar from flowers

In the context of the passage, the term "proboscis" refers to the long, tube-like structure that adult butterflies use to collect nectar from flowers. The proboscis acts like a straw, allowing the butterfly to suck up the sweet liquid from the flowers. This helps the butterfly feed and also serves the important role of pollination as they transfer pollen from one flower to another while feeding. The other choices are not the best answers because:
B) The process of molting and shedding the caterpillar's skin is not what "proboscis" refers to;
C) The final stage of a butterfly's life cycle is not related to the term "proboscis";
D) The delicate and suspended structure of the chrysalis is also not what "proboscis" refers to.

23. B) Larva (Caterpillar)

In the context of the passage, the stage of a butterfly's life cycle that involves the caterpillar shedding its outer skin multiple times to accommodate its increasing size is the "Larva" stage, also known as the caterpillar stage. As caterpillars grow, their outer skin becomes too tight, and they shed it in a process called "molting." This allows them to continue growing and getting bigger. The other choices are not the best answers because:

A) The "Egg" stage is when the butterfly lays eggs; C) The "Pupa (Chrysalis)" stage is when the caterpillar transforms into a butterfly inside the chrysalis; D) The "Adult (Butterfly)" stage is when the butterfly has fully developed wings and is ready to fly and reproduce.

24. D) They transfer pollen from one flower to another while feeding on nectar.
According to the information in the passage, butterflies are considered essential pollinators because they transfer pollen from one flower to another while feeding on nectar. This pollen transfer is a crucial process for plant reproduction, as it helps fertilize the flowers and allows them to produce seeds and fruit. The other choices are not the best answers because: A) The act of laying tiny eggs on plant leaves does not directly contribute to pollination; B) The remarkable transformation during metamorphosis is not related to their role as pollinators; C) The fact that they have strong jaws to munch on leaves and plants is related to their feeding behavior, but not specifically to pollination.

25. A) 1
In the context of the passage, the word "splits" refers to the action of the chrysalis breaking open. This matches the dictionary meaning "to break," as the chrysalis breaks open to allow the fully developed adult butterfly to emerge. The other choices are not the best answers because: B) "to end an emotional relationship" is not relevant to the context; C) "to jump into the air and then sit with legs apart" does not apply to the chrysalis opening; D) "to suffer from headache" is unrelated to the process described in the passage.

The Talking Bird, The Singing Tree, And The Golden Water

26. B) To observe what was transacting in the city
The emperor took night excursions through the city in order to observe and learn about what was happening in his kingdom. He wanted to gain knowledge of affairs and understand the lives of his subjects. This is evident from the passage where it is mentioned that he went out in disguise with his grand vizier to see what was transacting in the city. The other choices are not the best answers because: A) while he was accompanied by his trusty minister, the main purpose was to observe the city; C) attending his father's funeral rites was a separate event mentioned in the passage; D) becoming the sultan's chief cook is not mentioned as his purpose for the night excursions.

27. B) Their wishes
The three sisters in the story were discussing their wishes. Each sister was sharing her desires and what she would wish for if given the chance. This is evident from the passage where the sisters talk about their wishes: the eldest sister wishes to marry the sultan's baker, the second sister wishes to marry the sultan's chief cook, and the youngest sister wishes to become the emperor's queen-consort with specific characteristics for her future child. The other choices are not the best answers because they do not accurately reflect the content of their conversation as described in the passage.

28. C) To become the sultan's baker's wife

The eldest sister wished to become the sultan's baker's wife. In the passage, she expresses her wish to have the sultan's baker as her husband so that she could eat the sultan's bread, which is considered excellent. She says, "for then I shall eat my fill of that bread, which by way of excellence is called the sultan's." This indicates that her wish is to marry the sultan's baker to have access to the special bread. The other choices are not the best answers because they do not accurately represent the specific wish mentioned by the eldest sister.

29. A) To be the emperor's queen-consort and have a special son

The youngest and most beautiful sister wished to become the emperor's queen-consort and have a special son. In the passage, she takes a higher flight with her wish, saying, "I wish to be the emperor's queen-consort. I would make him father of a prince, whose hair should be gold on one side of his head, and silver on the other; when he cried, the tears from his eyes should be pearls; and when he smiled, his vermilion lips should look like a rosebud fresh-blown." This shows that her wish is for a grand and unique life as the emperor's queen, with a son possessing extraordinary qualities. The other choices are not the best answers because they do not accurately represent the specific wish mentioned by the youngest sister.

30. B) vizier

The word "vizier" in paragraph 2 signifies a high-ranking officer. In the passage, it mentions "attended by his grand vizier," which refers to a trusted minister who holds an important position in the emperor's court. The other choices are not the best answers because they do not specifically refer to a high-ranking officer in this context.

31. B) To observe the city's activities

Emperor Kosrouschah and his grand vizier disguise themselves and roam the city at night to observe what is happening in the city. This helps them gain a better understanding of the affairs and activities of the people in the city. The other choices are not the main reason stated in the passage. While engaging in adventures, finding suitable persons for important positions, or escaping from their duties may be secondary outcomes, the primary purpose mentioned is to observe the city's activities.

32. C) Her wish shows that she understands power.

The youngest sister's wish stands out from the wishes of her two elder sisters because her wish demonstrates an understanding of power and grandeur. While her elder sisters wish for more tangible and material things like being the wife of the sultan's baker or chief cook, the youngest sister's wish is for something much more significant and impressive - to become the emperor's queen-consort and have a special son with extraordinary qualities. Her wish reflects her understanding of authority, status, and the potential to have a significant impact, making it distinct from the more immediate desires of her sisters. The other choices do not capture the unique aspect of the youngest sister's wish as effectively.

33. B) The disguise ran so fast that the police could not catch it.

The word "disguise" means to change how you look. However, in the sentence "The disguise ran so fast that the police could not catch it," the word "disguise" is used incorrectly. Disguises are things people wear to look different, and they cannot run. The other choices use the word "disguise" correctly. In choice (A), it

www.math-knots.com | www.a4ace.com

talks about a "spy using a clever disguise," which is right. In choice (C), it talks about "wearing a colorful mask as a disguise," which is right. In choice (D), it talks about a "detective coming up with a new disguise," which is right. So, the best answer is choice (B) because it uses the word "disguise" incorrectly by saying that it ran fast.

34. C) The youngest sister

The youngest sister had the highest and most extravagant wish among the three sisters. While the eldest sister wished for the sultan's baker as her husband to eat his special bread, and the second sister wished to be the wife of the sultan's chief cook to enjoy excellent dishes, the youngest sister's wish was even grander. She wished to be the emperor's queen-consort and have a son with unique and amazing features, such as hair that is gold on one side and silver on the other, tears that turn into pearls, and vermilion lips that look like a fresh-blown rosebud. This wish stood out as more extravagant and imaginative compared to her sisters' wishes. The other choices are not correct because they do not accurately describe the differences in the sisters' wishes.

The Emperor's New Clothes

35. B) They were invisible to everyone.

In the passage, it is mentioned that the weavers claimed to weave clothes with the wonderful property of remaining invisible to everyone who was unfit for their office or who was extraordinarily simple in character. This unique quality of the clothes is the focus of the emperor's interest, as he believes that wearing these clothes would help him identify those who are unfit for their positions and distinguish the wise from the foolish. The other choices are not the best answers because they do not accurately capture the specific property of the clothes as described in the passage.

36. C) He wanted to distinguish wise people from foolish ones.

In the passage, it is mentioned that the emperor thought that if he had a suit made from the special cloth woven by the weavers, he could find out which men in his realms were unfit for their offices and also be able to distinguish the wise from the foolish. The emperor's main motivation for wanting the cloth was to use its unique property to identify individuals who were not suitable for their positions and to discern those who were wise. The other choices are not the best answers because they do not accurately capture the emperor's specific intention as described in the passage.

37. C) They stored silk and gold thread in their knapsacks.

In the passage, it is stated that the weavers asked for delicate silk and pure gold thread, which they then put into their own knapsacks. They pretended to work on the looms, but in reality, they were not weaving anything; they were simply storing the materials in their knapsacks. This is how they deceived the emperor and the people into believing that they were creating a special cloth with remarkable properties. The other choices are not the best answers because they do not accurately describe the weavers' actions as presented in the passage.

38. B) He worried that he might be considered a simpleton.
In the passage, it is mentioned that the emperor remembered that a simpleton or someone unfit for his office would be unable to see the cloth's manufacture. The emperor was concerned that if he couldn't see the cloth, it might indicate that he was unfit for his position. This is why he felt embarrassed about seeing the cloth himself and preferred sending someone else to assess it. The other choices do not accurately capture the emperor's specific concern and hesitation mentioned in the passage.

39. C) the act of thinking about or discussing something and deciding carefully.
In the context of paragraph 6, the word "deliberation" refers to the careful consideration and thought that the emperor puts into deciding who should be sent to assess the weavers' work. It indicates that the emperor is taking his time to think about the best course of action before making a decision.
The other choices do not accurately capture the specific meaning of "deliberation" as used in this context.

40. B) He couldn't see any cloth on the looms.
In paragraph 7, the old minister went to see the weavers' work, and he opened his eyes wide in surprise, realizing that he couldn't find any thread on the looms. This indicates that the weavers were not actually weaving any cloth despite their pretended efforts. The other choices are not accurate because there is no mention of the weavers diligently working on the looms, finishing their work, or producing cloth of beautiful colors and patterns.

41. A) Paragraph 1.
This paragraph tells us that the emperor loved new clothes so much that he spent all his money on them and didn't care about his soldiers or other activities. It shows that his focus was mainly on dressing up and displaying his attire. The other choices are incorrect because
B) Paragraph 2 introduces the weavers and their claim,
C) Paragraph 3 talks about the emperor's decision to have the special clothes woven, and
D) Paragraph 4 describes the weavers' actions, none of which directly express the emperor's fascination with clothes and disregard for other matters as much as A) Paragraph 1 does.

42. C) He thinks the minister is the wisest person in the city.
The passage mentions that the emperor considers the minister to be a man of sense and the most suitable person for the task. The emperor believes that the minister's wisdom and judgment will help him accurately evaluate the weavers' work. The other choices are incorrect because there is no indication that the minister has weaving skills (A), needs to learn the technique (B), or is being tested for loyalty and honesty (D).

The Little Mermaid

43. B) She has a fish tail instead of feet.
The passage describes that while the princess is beautiful with soft skin and deep blue eyes, her body ends in a tail like that of a fish. This is what sets her apart and makes her different from humans who have feet. The other choices (A, C, D) are not mentioned in the passage and are not characteristics of the youngest princess's body.

44. C) Bright blue-like flames of Sulphur
The passage describes the sand in the garden as being of bright blue color, resembling flames of Sulphur. This unique color adds to the beauty and uniqueness of the garden.
The other choices (A, B, D) are not mentioned in relation to the color of the sand in the garden.

45. C) They allowed themselves to be caressed by the princesses.
The passage mentions that when the great amber windows of the palace apartments were opened, fishes would swim into the rooms and allow themselves to be caressed by the little princesses. This interaction between the fishes and the princesses demonstrates a friendly and playful relationship.
The other choices (A, B, D) are not mentioned in relation to the fish's behavior in the palace apartments.

46. C) Paragraph 3
Paragraph 3 describes the Mer-king's palace, including details about its construction, such as walls of coral and high windows of amber, as well as the roof made of mussel-shells adorned with bright pearls. This paragraph provides a vivid depiction of the palace's appearance and its ornamental features. The other paragraphs (A, B, D) focus on different aspects of the story and do not provide a description of the palace.

47. C) Paragraph 6
Paragraph 6 provides a description of the garden in front of the palace, emphasizing the unique and vibrant colors of the flora, such as fiery red and dark blue trees with fruit that glitters like gold. It also describes the bright blue sand that forms the soil of the garden, creating a striking visual scene.
The other paragraphs (A, B, D) focus on different aspects of the story and do not provide a description of the garden.

48. B) The Mer-people appreciate the vivid and vibrant colors of nature, evident in their palace and garden.
The passage describes the Mer-people's palace with walls of coral, high pointed windows of amber, and a roof composed of mussel-shells with bright, glittering pearls. Additionally, the garden in front of the palace is depicted as full of fiery red and dark blue trees with golden fruit and bright blue sand. These details suggest that the Mer-people have a strong appreciation for vibrant and colorful aesthetics in their surroundings. The other choices (A, C, D) are not supported by the information provided in the passage.

www.math-knots.com | www.a4ace.com

49. **B) Her extravagant jewelry and attire showcase her wealth and opulence.**

The passage mentions that the Mer-king's mother wears twelve oysters on her tail, signifying her pride in her high birth and station. This detail, along with her extravagant adornments, suggests that she values her status and wealth. The other choices (A, C, D) do not accurately reflect the description of the Mer-king's mother's appearance and personality as portrayed in the passage.

50. **B) -le**

The correct answer is B) -le. The word 'sensible' contains the suffix -le, which is a common suffix used in English words to form adjectives. In this case, the suffix -le is added to the base word 'sens' to create the adjective 'sensible,' which means having good judgment or practical wisdom.

The other choices (A, C, D) are incorrect as they do not accurately identify the suffix in the word 'sensible.'

Made in the USA
Las Vegas, NV
07 July 2024